The Complete Photo Guide to
CLOTHING CONSTRUCTION

Creative Publishing international

First published in the United States of America by
Creative Publishing international, Inc., a member of
Quayside Publishing Group
400 First Avenue North
Suite 400
Minneapolis, MN 55401
1-800-328-3895
www.creativepub.com

Visit www.Craftside.Typepad.com for a behind-the-scenes peek at our crafty world!

ISBN: 978-1-58923-777-3

10 9 8 7 6 5 4 3 2 1

Library of Congress Cataloging-in-Publication Data available.

Copy Editor: Kari Cornell
Proofreader: Karen Levy
Cover Design: Creative Publishing international, Inc.
Page Layout: Laurie Young
Photographs: Gaby Moussa
Photo Styling: Christine Haynes

Printed in China

DEDICATION

For Mike

The Complete Photo Guide to
CLOTHING CONSTRUCTION

Creative Publishing
international

CONTENTS

Introduction

I love to sew. It is my passion, my love, my business, and my hobby. What I especially enjoy sewing are garments, particularly dresses. Learning to sew your own clothing can change a person. It teaches you to love and understand your body, it educates you on the work it takes to construct something you might buy without much thought, and it allows you to express yourself in a personal and unique way. It might sound like a stretch to say that sewing your own clothing can change the world, but it can lead to some profound conversations about a handmade or store-bought lifestyle.

Sewing, like cooking or any other craft, is much easier with the right tools and knowledge. I hope this book encourages you to try a few things for the first time, or to revisit a skill you might need to brush up on. I have included all the basic skills required for garment construction, and, for those of you who are ready, I've included some skills that are beyond basic, such as French seams and rolled hems.

At the end of every section you will find "Anatomy of a Garment" sidebars with photos of different garments—everything from shorts, to children's wear, to dresses—with lists highlighting all the skills and elements needed to construct each piece. Many people underestimate how many skills are necessary to assemble a "simple" dress. These examples shine a light on what goes into creating the clothing we wear every day.

I hope you enjoy the book and I look forward to hearing from you on my website or blog at www.ChristineHaynes.com. Happy sewing!

Anatomy of a Garment

Underststitching (1)
Invisible zipper (2)
Facings (3)

Flat buttons (4)
Gathering (5)
Hand stitched hem (6)

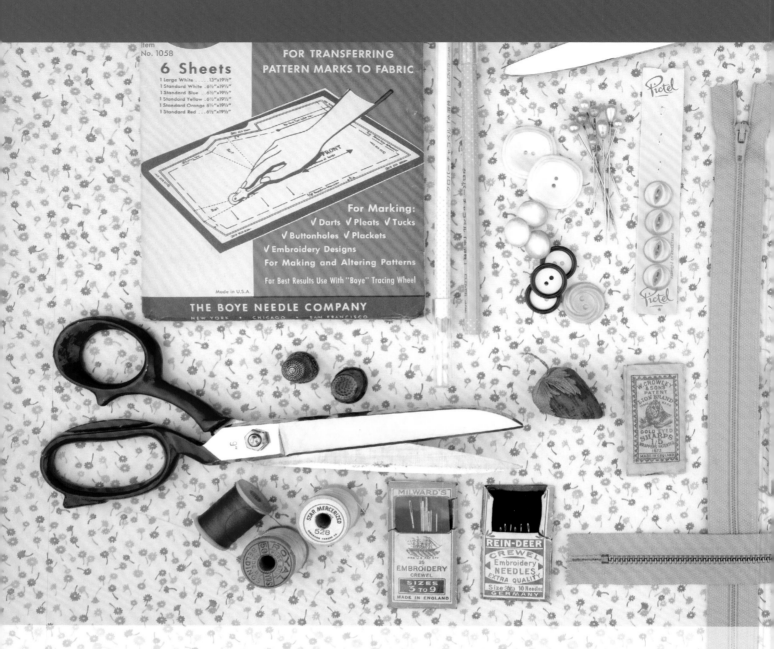

TOOLS OF THE TRADE

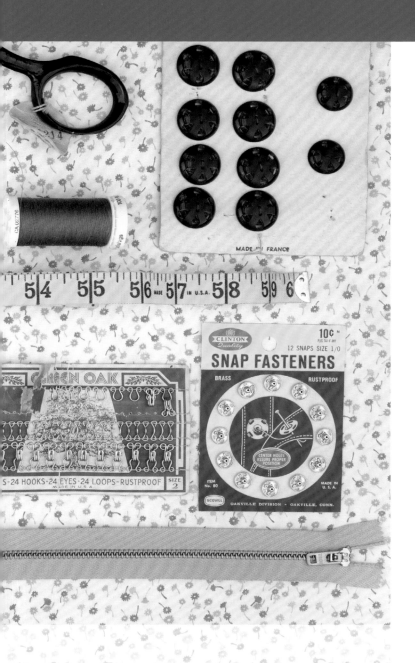

As with any hobby or craft, having the right tools will not only make the end result better, but it will also make the journey a much more enjoyable one. In this section, we explore all the key tools needed to get started with sewing, move you forward, and help you finish every garment on your to-do list. We begin with the most important tool, the sewing machine, and work our way through each item you might want to consider purchasing. There is no shortage of handy items on the market, but you certainly do not need all of them. In this section, I will suggest the best tools for the tasks at hand.

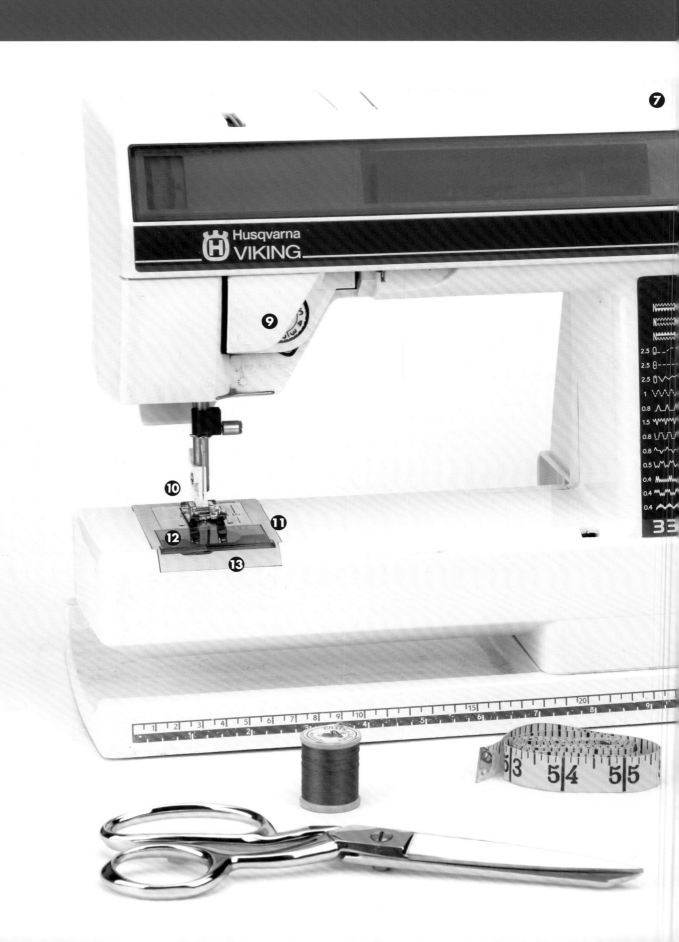

The Sewing Machine

The most important tool in your collection is your sewing machine. Machines can vary dramatically from the most basic to elaborate computerized machines, but what is most important is that your machine can do the basics well: the straight stitch, a zigzag stitch, and buttonholes. These are the key stitches you will use when assembling a garment, and even the most basic of machines should be able to offer you these choices.

Additional stitches that will come in handy are the three-step zigzag, a blind hem, and a stretch option for straight stitch sewing. These stitches will make it easier to sew certain elements, allow you more fabric choices, and provide additional options when finishing your garments.

Because every machine is different, I highly recommend reading your manual from cover to cover. If you purchased a used machine or have lost your manual over the years, most can be found on the Internet by searching for the make and model of your sewing machine. Even the most experienced sewer can learn a thing or two by reading what the manufacturer has written about your particular machine.

PARTS OF THE SEWING MACHINE

While all machines are different, most will have all of the following parts, although it's likely they will be in slightly different locations. The following parts are identified in the photo on page 10.

Hand Wheel (1)

When you turn the hand wheel toward you, you are manually making the same movement inside the machine as when you place your foot on the floor pedal. If you need to move forward at a stitch-by-stitch pace, turn this wheel toward you to do it manually. Avoid turning the hand wheel away from you when the sewing machine is threaded; this moves the threads in reverse, causing a thread knot and jam under the presser foot.

Power Cord and Foot Pedal (2)

Under the hand wheel you'll find a plug for the electrical power cord and the foot pedal cord. Some machines have two separate cords for the electricity and the foot pedal, while on other machines they are joined into one cord. Either way, the cord(s) plug in on the lower part of the side of the machine and are accompanied by the power switch, which also turns on an interior light to illuminate your sewing area. The foot pedal rests on the floor. Position it with the lower side facing you and press with your foot to power your machine. It works much like a car pedal; the harder you press on it, the faster the machine will go. The sensitivity of each pedal can take some getting used to.

Stitch Selection Dial (3)

On my machine, the stitch selection and stitch width share the same dial, but on yours the stitch selection may have its own dial or button. The stitch selection dial allows you to choose the stitch with which you'd like to sew. Some machines have many options, while others have only a few. Turn your knob or push your button to select the desired stitch, and then adjust your length and width accordingly.

Stitch Width Dial (4)

For straight stitch sewing, each machine will require you to adjust your stitch width so that the needle is in the "center" position. Note that all machines are different, and that the "center" position is not always in the center. Refer to your manual to determine the "center" position for your make and model, as this is what the seam allowance measurements are based upon. If you are not in the correct position, the seam allowance distance stated on the foot plate will not be accurate. For stitches that have side-to-side width to them, like a zigzag stitch, the stitch width dial sets your stitch from narrow to wide, and everything in between.

Stitch Length Dial (5)

The stitch length dial adjusts the length from stitch to stitch. For a straight stitch, the length is from each entry into the fabric. For a zigzag stitch, the length can be adjusted to match the width to create a variety of combinations of short and wide, long and narrow, long and wide, and so on. Your stitch length always needs to be adjusted based on the type and thickness of the fabric. Keep in mind that the heavier the fabric, the longer the stitch length should be.

Reverse Button (6)

All machines come with a button or switch to sew in reverse. The main reason to use this is for sewing a backstitch. Learn more about backstitching in the Sewing Machine Stitches section (page 62).

Thread Spool Pin (7)

The spool of thread rests on the spool pin. Some are horizontal with a cap to hold it in place, and some are vertical on the top of the machine. Many machines with vertical spool pins have a second pin alongside the first for dual thread topstitching with a twin needle. Check your manual to see if your machine has a preference for the unspooling direction of your thread.

Bobbin Winder (8)

It takes two threads to form a stitch. One of the threads is from the spool on the spool pin, and the other is from the bobbin. The bobbin rests under the foot plate, but first you must load it full of thread from the main spool. You will wind the thread onto the bobbin using the bobbin winder. On most machines, there is a dashed diagram to indicate how to run the thread from the main spool to your bobbin winder. If you are unsure, please refer to your machine's manual.

Tension Dial (9)

Behind the tension dial are metal discs that are engaged when the presser foot is lowered. These discs regulate the distribution of the thread from that point in the sewing machine to the needle. It is important that these are set correctly, or the machine might have too much thread going to the stitch, or too little, resulting in a stitch that is too loose or too tight. Always thread your machine with the discs open by raising your presser foot.

Presser Foot (10)

There are hundreds of presser feet options for every task under the sun. Your machine comes with an all-purpose foot, and likely a few additional specialty feet for zipper insertion, buttonholes, and more. Be sure to use the foot appropriate to the task at hand.

Foot Plate (11)

Under the presser foot is your foot plate. On this piece are measurements for seam allowance options. Some machines will have only lines and no numerical markings. To determine which line equals which measurement, reference your manual, or measure from the "center" needle position to each line with a small ruler or seam gauge.

Feed Dogs (12)

On your foot plate are channels with metal teeth poking above the plate. Those teeth are the feed dogs and they pull your fabric through the machine in time with the speed of the pedal or hand wheel. For the feed dogs to pull the fabric, the presser foot must always be lowered on top of the fabric so the pressure of the presser foot can hold the fabric in place as the feed dogs pull it through.

Bobbin (13)

The bobbin is the second spool of thread that forms your stitch. Once you have wound it full of thread on the bobbin winder, insert it into the casing that houses the bobbin. It is important to have the correct bobbin for your machine make and model; when purchasing additional bobbins, be sure to buy the size that fits your sewing machine.

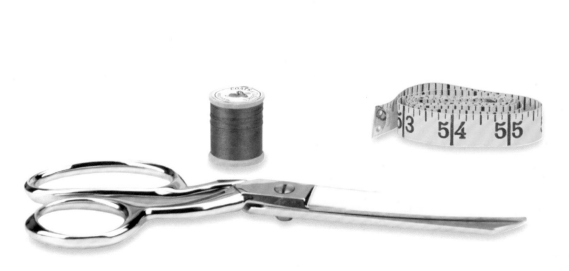

SEWING MACHINE FEET

Much like all other parts of your sewing machine, the different feet options are make and model specific, so reference your manual before investing in a specialty foot to ensure that you are getting the correct size for your machine. The same kind of foot can look dramatically differently from brand to brand, so know that not all feet of the same kind will look the same. I suggest purchasing your sewing machine parts from an authorized dealer for your machine brand so you know you have purchased the correct items.

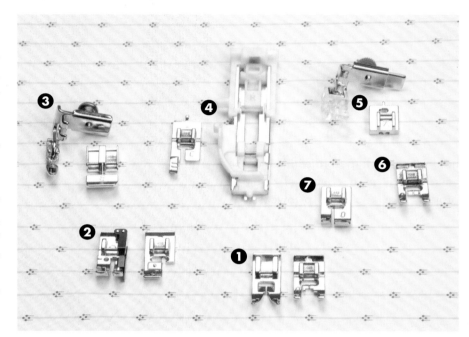

All-Purpose Foot (1)

The all-purpose foot is the one that was attached to your machine when you purchased it. This foot is to be used for basic sewing and will be the one you use most of the time.

Quarter-inch Seam Foot (2)

This foot assists in sewing a ¼" (6 mm) seam for a perfect finish. Often used in topstitching, the foot holds the fabric in place to provide professional-looking stitching.

Zipper Foot (3)

Some machines have a zipper foot that looks like half of a foot, while others have a space missing on both the right and the left sides with a bar down the middle. Both options allow you to move the needle very close to the teeth of the zipper.

Buttonhole Foot (4)

The smaller buttonhole foot is for a 4- or 5-step buttonhole, and the larger foot is for a 1-step buttonhole. The buttonhole foot has a space in the back where the machine can "measure" the size of the button and automatically adjust the size of the buttonhole.

Invisible or Concealed Zipper Foot (5)

The best way to sew an invisible zipper is to use the invisible zipper foot and allow the teeth of the zipper to ride in the channels on the underside of the foot. This makes for a very easy zipper insertion.

Decorative and Satin Stitch Foot (6)

This looks very much like an all-purpose foot, but it is usually shorter and the underside is cut away to ride smoothly over decorative stitches.

Blind Hem Foot (7)

This foot makes it easy to sew a blind hem—a hem in which one layer of the fabric is thicker than the other side—as one side of the foot is higher than the other.

SEWING MACHINE NEEDLES

Needles come in all shapes and sizes and some are machine or brand specific, so check your manual to see which needles will fit your machine. Anything sharp can dull, and machine needles are no exception. After one large project, like an entire dress, or a couple of small projects, like a tote and pillowcase, the needle will begin to dull, resulting in uneven and dropped stitches. Do not be afraid to switch out needles often, as it is the key to good stitching. Here are some of the more common needle types and sizes you will encounter when sewing clothing.

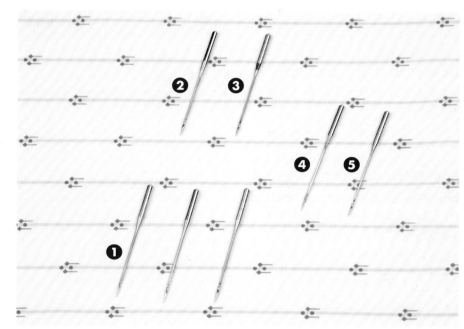

All-Purpose Universal Needles (1)

The all-purpose needle is exactly as it sounds: it will sew through most things. That means that it is the master of none, but it is a good versatile choice if you'd rather just keep one type of needle on hand. If you know in advance that you want to sew with woven fabric or knits, it is best to use fabric-specific needles, as listed below.

The heavier the needle, the higher the number, and vice versa. Heavier needles are for thicker fabrics, and lighter needles are for lighter fabrics. An 80/12 is ideal for medium-weight woven fabric, with the heavier and lighter varieties landing on either side.

Wedge Point Leather Needle (2)

A wedge point needle has a thicker and heavier beveled point at the end so it can pierce through leather and vinyl fabrics.

Microtex Needle (3)

A microtex needle is finer than an all-purpose needle and has a sharper point, making it best for woven fabrics.

Stretch Needle (4)

Stretch needles have a ball-point tip that is slightly rounded so it won't break through the threads of knit fabrics.

Jersey Needle (5)

Like stretch needles, jersey needles are ball-point tipped, but are designed for synthetic stretch fabrics like swimsuit wear and spandex.

Cutting Tools

When cutting anything, it is important to use the correct tool for the job. Otherwise, you might accidently cut something you did not intend to, or unknowingly dull a tool during a task that would have been better suited for a different cutting device.

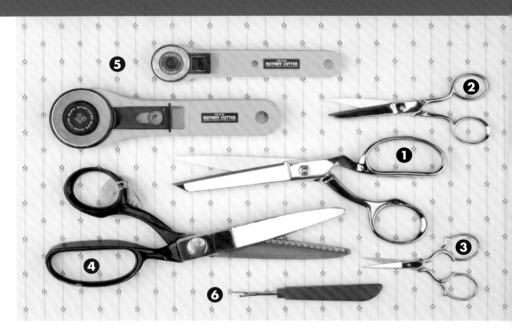

BENT-HANDLED SCISSORS (1)

One of the most important items in your tool kit is a quality pair of 8" (20.3 cm) fabric scissors. Every step of sewing relies upon accurate cutting, and cutting correctly is much easier with sharp scissors. The bent handle of these scissors will allow the lower blade to glide along your cutting surface, keeping your project flat for more precise cuts. Reserve these only for cutting fabric and they will stay sharp for many months. Choose a pair of inexpensive scissors to use when cutting patterns so you won't dull your fabric scissors. When it comes time to re-sharpen your fabric scissors, be sure to take them to a professional sharpener so the blades are cared for properly.

TRIMMING SCISSORS (2)

When it comes time to trim and grade the seam allowances of your garment, it's a bit tricky to do this correctly with large 8" (20.3 cm) scissors. Having a sharp pair of 5" (12.7 cm) scissors in your kit will prevent mistakes and allow you to cut small areas with ease.

EMBROIDERY SCISSORS (3)

Even if you are sewing and not doing embroidery, these little 3" (7.6 cm) scissors are perfect for clipping threads while at your sewing machine or other fine detailed clipping.

PINKING SCISSORS (4)

Pinking scissors have blades with triangle points on them, resulting in a zigzag cut, which can be used for both functional and decorative purposes. Pinking sheers are a quick and easy way to finish seams, because when most fabrics are cut with pinking scissors, the zigzag edge prevents the fabric from fraying.

ROTARY CUTTERS (5)

Typically one thinks of rotary cutters for quilting, but they can be extremely useful in garment sewing as well. Rotary blades and cutters come in a variety of sizes, with the most typical being 24 mm, 45 mm, and 60 mm. The blades are round razor blades and must be used on a self-healing cutting mat to preserve both your table underneath and the sharpness of the blade.

SEAM RIPPER (6)

The seam ripper is your tool for undoing any stitches that need to be removed. A good seam ripper has a small point to get underneath your stitch with ease and a sharp bevel for cutting the stitch. I prefer a seam ripper with a long handle, as it can be held firmly.

Pins

There are many types of pins on the market, so choosing the right ones for your specific project can be very confusing. It's important to match the correct point and weight of pin to your fabric type to prevent the pins from marring the fabric and leaving behind a hole that needs to be repaired.

QUILTING PINS (1)

Quilting pins have a thicker metal shaft and a large plastic ball at the top so you can see them easily while quilting. These are good for heavier fabrics in garment construction; just be careful not to press on them with your iron because the plastic balls will melt.

GLASS HEAD PINS (2)

Glass head pins are the best for all-purpose garment sewing, as the metal shaft is thinner, leaving behind a smaller hole, and the glass heads will not melt under the heat of an iron.

BALL-POINT PINS (3)

When working with knits you want to be sure to use all ball-point pins and needles. The point at the end is slightly rounded to prevent breaking the threads of the stretchy fabric. Not all are made with glass balls, so make sure you know whether you have glass or plastic prior to pressing on them with an iron.

SILK PINS (4)

Silk is the finest of fabrics and you want a small metal shaft on your pin to ensure that you leave only the smallest possible hole behind. These are made exclusively for that purpose and work great on all silks and similar fabrics.

SOFT PIN CUSHIONS (5)

Pin cushions come in all shapes and sizes including the classic tomato. These are useful for keeping your pins in place and some come with an emery-filled strawberry to keep your pins sharp and clean.

MAGNETIC PIN CUSHION (6)

A magnetic pin cushion is an easy way to keep your pins tidy and is great to use while sewing because it will catch your pins without you having to take your focus off the sewing machine. Magnetic cushions are also great for cleaning up spilled pins because the magnet will gather them up quickly.

Hand Sewing Tools

Even though you are using a sewing machine for construction, there are multiple situations when a hand sewing needle is helpful. As you embark on a project, you'll discover that a hand sewing needle is useful for both decorative and functional applications.

EMBROIDERY CREWEL NEEDLES (1)

Crewels tend to have a larger and longer eye for easy threading. They are medium to long in length and have sharp points, making them perfect for embroidery work.

MILLINERS (2)

Milliners are medium to long in length with a fine point. They are perfect for all-purpose stitching where a longer length is necessary, such as when basting by hand.

SHARPS (3)

Sharps are the most all-purpose needle and are medium in length. They have a slightly rounded eye and come in a range of sizes, appropriate for a wide variety of fabric types.

THIMBLES (4)

The thimble is a small cap worn on your fingers when sewing by hand. It protects your fingers from the end of the hand sewing needle as you push the needle and thread through fabric. Thimbles come in a variety of sizes and are usually made from metal or soft flexible plastic.

BEESWAX (5)

Running your thread through beeswax adds strength and smoothness to your thread while sewing by hand. Always test the wax on a scrap because some will stain fine fabrics.

NEEDLE THREADERS (6)

A needle threader is a quick and easy way to thread the eye of a hand sewing needle. Place the needle over the end of the metal wire, insert the thread through the wire, then pull the needle off the wire and the thread will be through your needle's eye.

Pressing Tools

The best way to elevate any garment is by quality pressing, so having the proper equipment on hand to achieve a polished finish is as important to your sewing kit as construction tools.

IRON (1)

To give a professional look to every garment you make, press it well. This is easy to do with a quality iron that has multiple heat settings for different kinds of fabrics and a steam option for extra heat if necessary. Keep the iron clean by using an iron cleaner on it once a month so debris from a previous project does not end up on future projects.

PRESSING CLOTHS (2)

Pressing cloths are used for a few different purposes and made from a variety of fabrics. You would use a pressing cloth between your ironing board and fusible interfacing as well as between the fusible interfacing and your iron to prevent the interfacing adhesive from getting on your iron or ironing board. Muslin that is 100 percent cotton is perfect for this purpose. Wools, cotton canvas, silk organza, and cotton flannel are great choices for preventing iron marks when pressing onto fragile or specific fabrics.

SLEEVE BOARD (3)

The sleeve board is essentially a mini ironing board, which is perfect for pressing small items that have been sewn in the round. Insert the board into a sleeve, pant leg, or other similar shape to press the top layer without pressing the under layer.

SEAM ROLL (4)

Much like a sleeve board, the seam roll is used to prevent pressing the underside of a garment while pressing the top layer. It's perfect for slipping into pant legs, under zippers, or any other top layer you want to press without pressing the underside.

PRESSING HAM (5)

A pressing ham's job is to take the place of a three-dimensional object that you have built shaping for in your garment, such as a bust dart or sleeve cap. Place the ham under the fabric to fill in the gap that your body will fill when wearing and press around to shape the garment.

IRONING BOARD (NOT PICTURED) (6)

Whether it is a full-size or small tabletop ironing board, a pressing surface is an absolute must for garment construction. While sewing there will be pressing between nearly every stitch, as well as pressing all the fabric at the start and the final finished garment at the end. All of this is much easier with a proper spot for ironing.

Marking Tools

There are a number of situations when marking on the fabric is necessary, so picking the correct method for your application and fabric type is important. Always try out marking tools on a scrap of the fabric you're using to make sure it behaves the way you want before using it on the finished item.

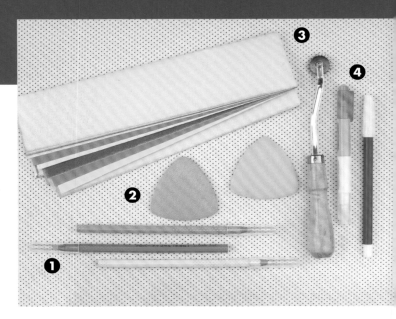

CHALK PENCILS (1)

Tailor's chalk comes in a variety of forms, including chalk pencils. Some are specifically water soluble while others are not. I prefer the water-soluble versions, because then I know it will come out of my fabric, but it's always a good idea to test them first. There are also mechanical chalk pencils that can give you a more precise line.

CHALK TRIANGLE WEDGES (2)

Another form of chalk is the triangle wedge. These are perfect for quick broad strokes, especially on a muslin surface when it's not necessary for the chalk to wash out of the fabric. They are available in white, red, blue, and yellow. Choose a color that will show up clearly on the fabric you are marking.

TRACING PAPER AND TRACING WHEEL (3)

Place your tracing paper on top of your fabric, run over it with your tracing wheel, and the chalk coating on the paper will transfer to the fabric. As with the chalk, look for tracing paper that is wax-free and will wash out with water.

MARKING PENS (4)

Marking pens are like chalk pencils in that they are perfect for making precision markings. Most are water or air soluble so they are erased with water or over time as exposed to the air. Marking pens come in a variety of colors but are best suited for lighter colored fabrics, because they usually do not show up well on dark colors.

Measuring Tools

Precision sewing is achieved through a series of steps made with the right tools, none of which are more important than your measuring tools. These are the tools that you will use to mark where to stitch, where to cut, and what size to make the garment pieces. All of these are critical steps in garment construction.

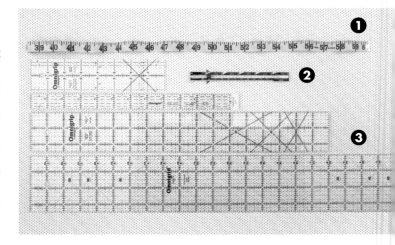

TAPE MEASURE (1)

In order to sew garments, you need accurate body measurements. The best tool for precisely measuring your body is a fiberglass flexible tape measure. The fiberglass will not shrink or stretch and is flexible enough to get around all the body's curves.

SEAM GAUGE (2)

The seam gauge is perfect for small measuring tasks like marking pivots, buttonholes, hems, pleats, and more. This is one of the best tools for precision sewing in your tool kit. Move the stopper up and down to the measurement of your choice and use the top to make your mark.

CLEAR RULERS (3)

Clear plastic rulers let you see through the measurements to your fabric below, allowing you to make sure it is properly lined up. Many of the rulers have diagonal lines that are helpful for cutting on the bias and at other angles. Choose a thick ruler if you are using a rotary cutter, as it will provide a defined ridge along which to run yourw blade.

Other Tools

In addition to the commonly known list of tools, there are a few others that can really come in handy during your garment making. These items are there to help when you may not have realized you needed it.

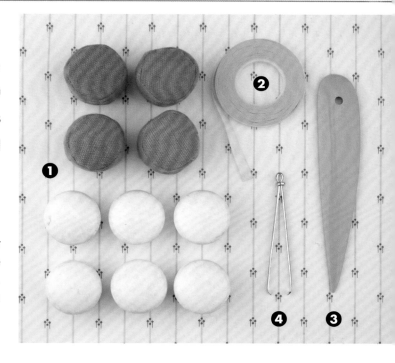

PATTERN WEIGHTS (1)

Pattern weights are a great alternative to pinning your pattern to your fabric, especially when using a delicate fabric that might be flawed with the piercing of a pin. Pattern weights are also helpful for quick cutting with a rotary cutter.

BASTING TAPE (2)

Water-soluble basting tape is much like basting with thread, but is handy in places where thread is not enough or the spot is too awkward to sew. Make perfect flat-fell seams and sew flawless zippers with the help of this handy tool.

POINT TURNER (3)

The point turner has a pointed end that is perfect for poking out corners, but not sharp enough to break through the seam or cut threads. Use on collars, right angles, and all similar spots. Use the curved edge for pushing out small cured seams like those on a collar or neckline.

BODKIN (4)

A bodkin is a pair of tweezers with a locking ring that holds the tweezers closed. These are perfect for feeding elastic or a drawstring through a casing. Open the bodkin, place the elastic between the teeth, and lock the ring to hold it in place.

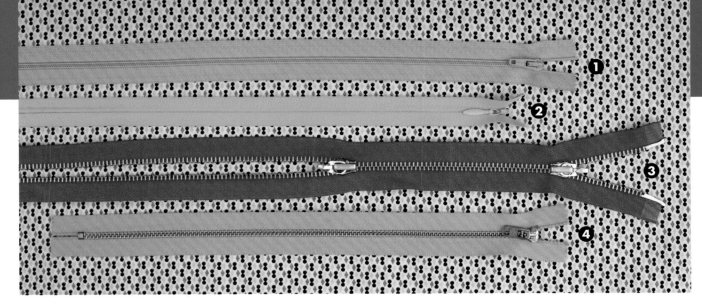

Closures

Few garments made of woven fabric can get on and off the body without the assistance of a closure like a button, zipper, snap, or Velcro. It is important to familiarize yourself with what each closure looks like, what it works best for, and how to use it. Here you will get to know the differences, then later in the book, you will learn how to use them.

ZIPPERS

Zippers come in a wide range of sizes, shapes, and colors. The zipper is often a practical choice, but it can also add aesthetic interest or decoration. The decision to match the zipper to the project or not is much like the choice to match thread or not. Technically speaking, matching is better, but as sewing is a creative venture, choosing to use a contrasting color is entirely up to you.

Regular Zipper (1)

Used in an extremely wide range of projects, the regular zipper with plastic teeth is the most common zipper on the market. It can be shortened by simply cutting the bottom and zigzag stitching over the teeth to create a new bottom stopper.

Invisible Zipper (2)

An invisible zipper is exactly that—when inserted into a seam properly. The only part of the zipper that will show is the top pull. It's perfect for side seams and back seams on finer garments when you do not want to draw any attention to the seam. Most have plastic teeth, but some metal versions are still on the market.

Separating Zipper (3)

A separating zipper can be pulled from either end to open completely. Used mostly in sportswear, jackets, and bags, these are typically more heavy duty than a regular zipper and can be found in both plastic and metal versions.

Metal Zipper (4)

More heavy duty than a plastic regular zipper, a metal zipper is constructed the same, but with durable metal teeth and pull. Great for more sturdy applications or for aesthetic interest, these brass zippers are most common in sewing jeans. When shortening, sew a new stopper by sewing by hand instead of with your sewing machine's zigzag stitch.

BUTTONS

Buttons come in more options than you can even dream about and it is likely that a button stash will develop in your tool kit. Buttons are usually functional, but always decorative, whether intentional or not. Consider using a contrasting color, a mix of buttons, or something vintage. This is one of the most personal choices you make in garment construction, so use it to reflect the spirit of the outfit and your personal taste.

Flat Buttons

Flat buttons, or sew-through buttons, have two or four holes through the face of the button for securing to your garment. They come in every possible shape and size, material and color. They are the most common buttons on the market and can be used for an extremely wide range of projects.

Shank Buttons

Shank buttons are like flat buttons, except instead of having a hole through the face of the button, they have a piece on the underside with a hole through it that you use to secure the button to the garment. These can be used for many projects, and are especially great for thick fabric garments like jackets.

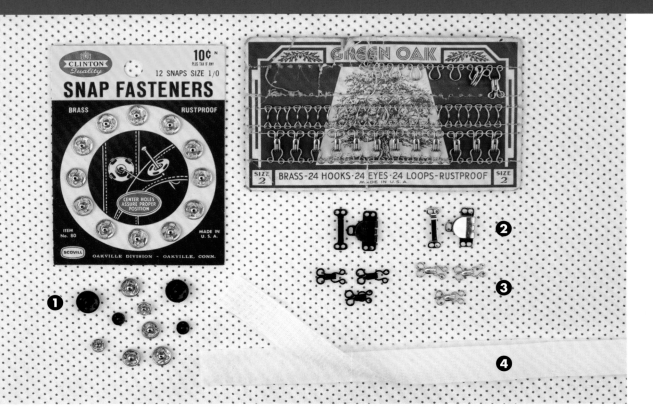

OTHER CLOSURES

In addition to buttons and zippers, there are many other ways to close a seam. Many of these are used in conjunction with buttons and zippers, but sometimes are used independently.

Snaps (1)

Snaps are made of two parts, a socket and a ball, which lock together. Each side is sewn to opposite sides of the fabric and then pushed together to lock, forming an invisible closure.

Waistband Hook and Eye (2)

Waistband hook-and-eye sets are flat to keep the front of the garment, typically a skirt or trousers, completely flat. These are usually used when you want an invisible finish instead of a button.

Hook and Eye (3)

Traditional hook-and-eye sets are made of metal wire and consist of two parts, one that is a flat loop and another that is curved up to hook under the loop. These are used often in areas where you want to close something in a discreet way, such as at the top of a zipper at the back of the neck, or at the waist on a shirtwaist dress between buttons.

Velcro (4)

Velcro nylon tape can be used in items when you want quick release, such as in action wear or children's clothing. Velcro comes in sew-in, iron-on, and glue-backed versions and in a wide range of color choices.

Thread

There are numerous types of thread on the market, and it is important to match the type of thread with your project, purpose, and fabric type. Typically, matching the content of the fabric with the content of the thread is best. For example, if you are using a fabric made of natural fibers, use a natural fiber thread as well so the final treatment and pressing do not contradict either the fabric or the thread. The importance of thread is not to be underestimated, as it is the fiber that is holding everything together.

COTTON-WRAPPED POLYESTER THREAD (1)

Cotton-wrapped polyester thread is an all-purpose choice that is commonly found in fabric stores worldwide. The polyester center is wrapped with cotton, making it a good, basic thread for a variety of uses.

COTTON THREAD (2)

Cotton thread is perfect for sewing with natural fibers such as cotton and linen. It holds up well to a hot iron and some brands have silk finishing for smooth application for gathering, basting, and hand finishing.

ELASTIC THREAD (3)

Elastic thread is used in the sewing machine bobbin for shirring by machine. Be sure to wind the elastic thread by hand onto your bobbin without stretching it.

SILK THREAD (4)

Silk thread is perfect when sewing with silk and other fine fabrics, as well as with wool for tailoring because it is easily molded into shape with an iron. It is also great for hand basting, as it does not leave marks behind.

POLYESTER THREAD (5)

Polyester thread is ideal when sewing with man-made synthetic fibers. Most have a bit of a sheen that will be visible on the finished garment. Because it is synthetic, be careful when pressing; polyester thread will melt and break under the heat of a hot iron.

CONE THREAD (6)

Cone thread spools are used in serger or overlocking machines and come in a variety of content. These are not suitable for a straight stitch machine unless a thread stand is used.

Notions

Trims, elastic, piping, ribbons, and lace are a few of the notions that can be used in sewing for both decorative and functional purposes. Each comes in an enormous range of content, size, color, and shape, so consult your pattern to make sure you are using the correct item in your project.

LACE (1)

Lace trim is a nice touch on the hem of a skirt or dress. Lace can be found in silk, rayon, cotton, and polyester in nearly every width, color, and style. Some come pre-gathered and others are flat.

SATIN RIBBON (2)

Polyester satin ribbon can be used for many decorative purposes, but note that it is synthetic and will not take to all situations. Some are double-faced so they are shiny on both sides, while others are only polished on the facing and dull on the back.

WOVEN RIBBON (3)

Unlike a printed ribbon, which is plain on one side and printed on the other, the print on woven ribbon is created by a series of woven threads. When deciding where to use woven ribbon, keep in mind that the back is typically not seen, so plan accordingly.

CORDING (4)

Cording comes in a range of colors and material. Some are made of twisted cables of polyester, satin, or cotton and can be sewn directly onto a garment in a decorative style. Other cording is plain white or black cotton and is sewn into strips of bias tape to be used when creating your own corded piping.

GROSGRAIN RIBBON (5)

Both decorative and practical, grosgrain ribbon made of polyester, cotton, or rayon can be found in a wide range of widths and colors. Sew it onto the facing of an outfit as a trim detail, or use it inside your dress as a waist stay.

VELVET RIBBON (6)

Velvet ribbon is luxurious and is available in silk or cotton in a range of colors and widths. The pile on velvet will crush when pressed, so be extra careful when ironing on or around this trim.

SILK RIBBON (7)

Silk ribbon is beautifully delicate and makes a lovely addition to any garment. This trim is made in every color and width and is usually only used for decorative purposes.

ELASTIC (8)

Elastic is used liberally in garment construction in waist seams, sleeve hems, and necklines. The most common colors of elastic are white and black, but decorative colors and prints are also on the market for times when you'd like to use exposed elastic at the waist. Widths of elastic range from very thin to very wide. Most elastic is made from rubber and is available in either braided or woven varieties.

HEM TAPE (9)

Hem tape is 100 percent polyester and is available in both fusible and sew-in versions. The sew-in version is sewn to the hem of a garment, folded into the wrong side, and used to sew to the inside instead of the garment hem. The fusible type is treated the same way, except the first step is to fuse the tape with an iron instead of sewing it with a machine.

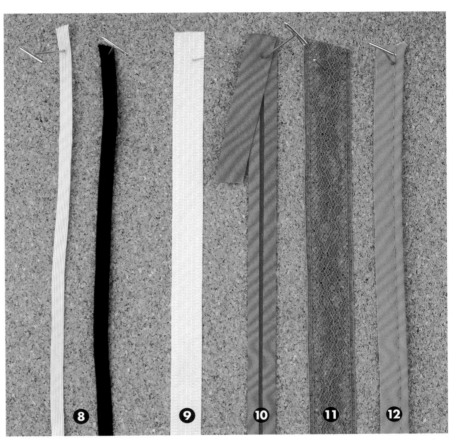

DOUBLE-FOLD AND SINGLE-FOLD BIAS TAPE (10)

Bias tape is made of strips of fabric cut on the bias, then sewn together into long strips. Each edge is folded into the center to form single-fold bias tape. To form double-fold bias tape, the strip is folded again down the center, with the first two folds trapped inside. These are used for a variety of edge finishing or for decorative trimming and come in a range of colors. Store-bought packages are usually a polyester-cotton blend, or you can construct your own from your fabric of choice.

LACE HEM TAPE (11)

Exactly like regular hem tape, lace hem tape is available in both sew-in and fusible varieties in a wide range of colors and is used to hem a garment. Insert it the same way as regular hem tape.

CORDED PIPING (12)

Corded piping is bias tape with cording sewn inside that you sew into a seam. It is a great way to add definition to interesting seam lines and can elevate the simplest of garments. Premade corded piping is usually a polyester-cotton blend, or you can make your own from a matching or contrasting fabric from your garment.

Anatomy of a Garment

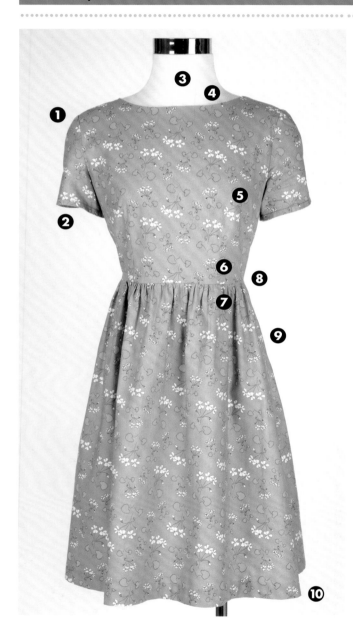

Set-in sleeves (1)	Waist darts (6)
Double fold sleeve hem (2)	Gathering (7)
Invisible zipper (3)	Seam grading (8)
Understitching (4)	In-seam pockets (9)
Bust darts (5)	Hand stitched hem (10)

Understitching (1)	Shank buttons (5)
Topstitching (2)	Pin tucks (6)
Bias binding sleeveless finishing (3)	Bust darts (7)
	Release pleats (8)
Buttonholes (4)	Double fold shirt hem (9)

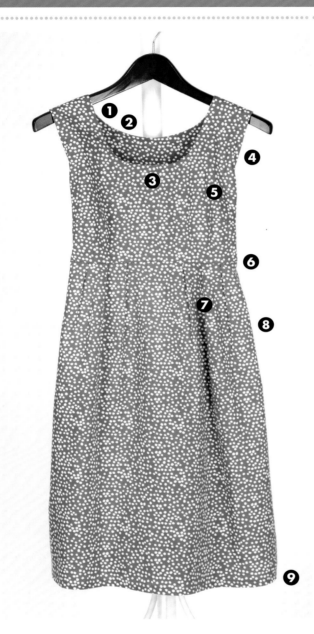

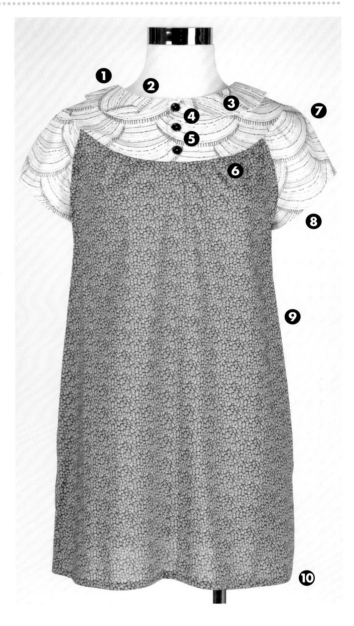

Clipping curves (1)	Bust darts (5)
Understitching (2)	Elastic shirring (6)
Topstitching (3)	Knife pleats (7)
Bias binding sleeveless	In-seam pockets (8)
finishing (4)	Double fold dress hem (9)

Flat collar (1)	Gathering (6)
Seam grading (2)	Raglan sleeves (7)
Topstitching (3)	Double fold sleeve hem (8)
Buttonholes (4)	In-seam pockets (9)
Flat buttons (5)	Double fold dress hem (10)

PATTERNS, FABRIC, AND YOUR BODY

Before you start sewing, it is important to choose the right pattern, know how to read it, match the pattern with the correct fabric type, and cut it well. These might seem like they are not as important as sewing straight, but they are the building blocks that will set you up for excellence when it is time to construct your new garment. In this chapter, you will learn how to start your next project with well-thought-out intention.

Sewing Patterns

There are many sewing pattern companies on the market. Some are big companies that create a wide range of patterns, from garments to crafts; others specialize in a certain body type; and some companies focus on a certain aesthetic style. No matter how different they all are, most follow basic guidelines to achieve a certain amount of consistency. Learning how to read the pattern properly is the first step to creating a quality finished garment.

HOW TO READ THE PATTERN ENVELOPE

Pattern Number (1)

All patterns are identified by a four digit number.

Sizing (2)

Look for a list of sizes included in the pattern on the front of the pattern envelope. Be sure to check the size chart on the back prior to purchasing to ensure that your size is included.

Brand Name (3)

Every pattern company displays their name somewhere on the front of the envelope.

Design Views (4)

Some patterns come with more than one design option for a particular garment. These are called "views" and are labeled with either letter or number notations.

Description (5)

On the back of the pattern envelope is a brief description of what the garment is like and how each view is different from the another.

Difficulty Rating (6)

Most pattern companies include some type of rating to give you an idea of how difficult the pattern will be to sew. Note that this rating is subjective and can vary between pattern companies. Some patterns labeled "easy" include elements like buttonholes, zippers, and other things that might not be considered "beginner."

Fabric Suggestions (7)

Not all projects are well suited for all fabric types. The pattern company suggests types of fabric that will work best for the particular garment. Usually these fabrics are listed from easiest to most difficult to work with.

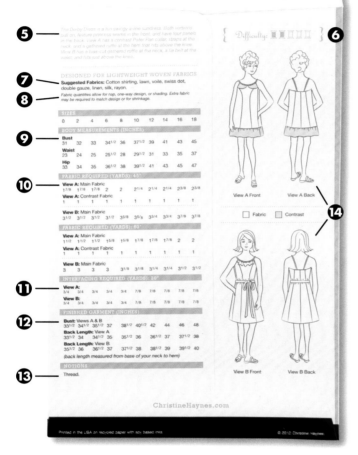

Size Chart (9)

Pattern companies each use their own sizing and none of these sizes have any relationship to the sizing used in ready-to-wear garments. So if you are used to wearing a certain size in a shop, do not expect that you can just cut the same size in your pattern, as it is very likely that the measurements are different. Compare your body measurements to the size chart to determine which size to make.

Fabric Requirements (10)

This chart breaks down by size, view, and fabric width, and lists how much yardage you need to make the item.

Interfacing Requirements (11)

Much like the fabric, if your project calls for interfacing, it likely is listed along with the fabric, based on the width of the bolt and your chosen size.

Finished Garment Measurements (12)

All pattern companies have finished garment measurements somewhere within the pattern. Some print it on the envelope back, some on the instruction sheet, and others on the patterns themselves. This is important, as it tells you the end size of the garment.

Notions (13)

This section lists all the other items needed to complete the garment, including thread, elastic, zippers, and buttons.

Detailed Illustrations (14)

No matter what drawings or photographs are on the front of the envelope, the back contains detailed drawings so you can see the seam lines, zippers, gathering, and more.

Directional Note (8)

Some pattern companies calculate their fabric quantities with all the pieces going head to toe in the same direction, and some do not. This is important to note if you have a one-way directional print, nap, or shading on your fabric, as you would want all of those items going the same way on your finished garment. If the pattern states that it allows for nap and directional prints, you know that the quantities listed will work for any type of fabric. But if you have directional fabric, and the pattern does not allow for nap and directional prints, then you will have to lay out your pieces and recalculate the quantity needed for your chosen size.

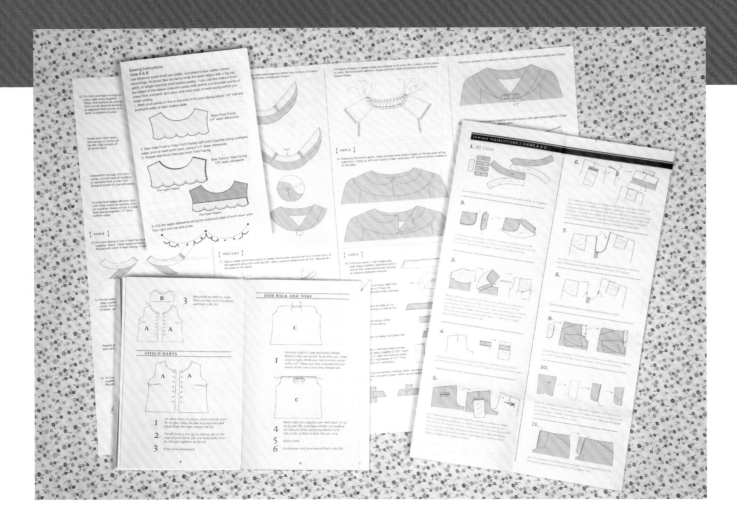

PATTERN INSTRUCTIONS

Pattern instructions can range from detailed booklets with clear illustrations to minimal descriptions and drawings. If looking for a beginner project, look for those labeled "learn to sew" or a similar phrase that indicates that the designer is not only teaching how to make the item, but also providing detailed, step-by-step instructions. Regardless of the level of difficulty, inside the pattern envelope is an instruction sheet or booklet that will contain most of the same information listed below.

PATTERN INVENTORY

This list of all the pattern pieces and shapes lets you know which you need to cut to create your desired view.

Layout Diagrams

These explain how to lay each piece onto the fabric to ensure all the pieces will fit on the fabric quantity suggested on the envelope. Remember to follow along with the correct view and size. If you are working with a directional fabric, also look for a chart that shows how to arrange the pattern pieces for directional fabrics.

Instruction Illustrations

Follow your view choice from step to step to construct the garment. If you are stuck on a step, consult a glossary, also often included on the instruction sheet.

Seam Allowance

Each pattern company follows a different seam allowance, though the standard is ⅝" (1.5 cm). Before you begin sewing, make note of the seam allowance on your instruction sheet.

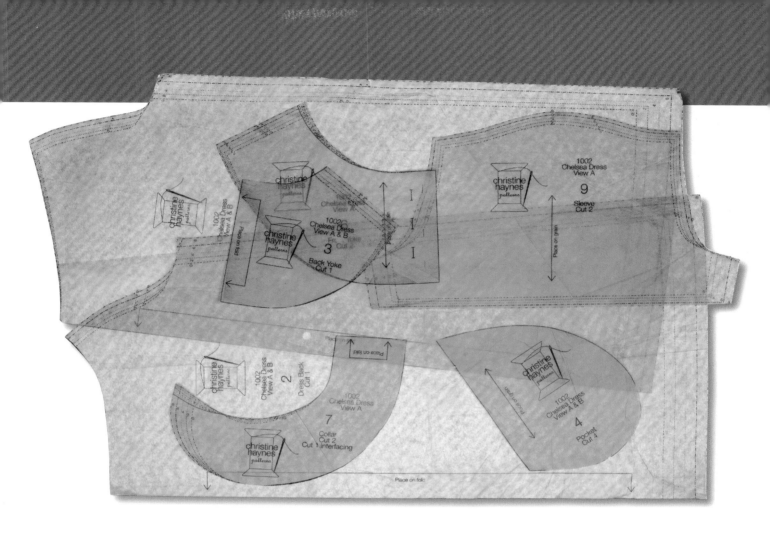

PATTERN MARKINGS

Decoding the meaning of all the marks on a pattern piece is a very important step. These marks instruct you on where to place the pattern piece, what marks to leave behind on your fabric, and where shaping occurs.

Pattern Name, Number, View, and Quantity to Cut

The following information is listed on every pattern piece: the name of the company, the pattern's four digit number, the view you are using, and a quantity to cut. The name and number ensure that if your pattern pieces somehow become separated from the envelope, you will know which pattern they are from. The quantity to cut tells you how many you will need of that piece in fabric, lining, and interfacing for your desired view.

(continued)

Grainline

The pattern piece must be "on grain" with the threads of the fabric in order for it to hang, move, stretch, and wear correctly. Always make sure that your grainline is parallel to the selvage of your fabric.

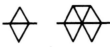

Notches

These triangles are to be cut either outside of your pattern piece or into the seam allowance. If your seam allowance is the standard ⅝" (1.5 cm), you have enough room to cut into the pattern. If it is smaller, be cautious and cut outside the shape.

Seam Line or Stitching Line

Not many pattern companies include these, but you might encounter them from time to time, especially on a vintage pattern. This is the actual line on which you will sew based on the seam allowance included.

Cutting Line

After you have selected the garment size, follow the line for your specific size. Most pattern companies have a minimum of three sizes per envelope; some have as many as ten, so be sure to follow the correct line for your chosen size. Cut just outside the line, and be sure to keep the clipped portion for future reference.

Lengthen or Shorten Line

If you need to lengthen or shorten the piece at a specific spot, the pattern designer indicates on the pattern pieces exactly where to make this adjustment.

Darts

Darts are areas of the fabric that will be folded for shaping. These are typically at the bust, waist, and upper neck.

Place on Fold Line

This edge of the pattern piece is to be placed on the fold of your fabric, making it easy to cut out a mirror image at the same time.

Circle Dots

Pattern companies will use circle dots, triangles, or squares to indicate construction details like pleating, end of the stitching line, or other steps that are explained on the instruction sheet.

Zipper Placement

The zipper placement line indicates where the zipper should be inserted into the garment based on the size of the zipper required.

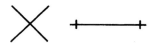 

Button and Buttonhole Placement

For garments with button closures, placement for buttonholes will be marked with lines on one side of the pattern piece. An X on the other side of the pattern piece indicates where the buttons should be attached.

Tucks

Transfer any tuck lines marked on the pattern pieces to the right side of the garment to indicate where the tucks should be sewn in place.

Hem Line

This line shows you where to sew the hem based on the pattern's hem allowance.

SEAM ALLOWANCE

Seam allowance is the distance between where you sew and the raw edge of the fabric. It is the invisible line around each pattern piece. Each project you sew has a set seam allowance built into it, and it is important that you sew at that seam allowance, or your pieces will not line up properly.

The most common and universally used seam allowance in garment construction is ⅝" (1.5 cm). Note that even if an entire project is sewn at a set seam allowance, specific seams might be changed to have a smaller seam allowance, especially around necklines or on details like bows and belts, so pay attention to the instructions as they guide you along.

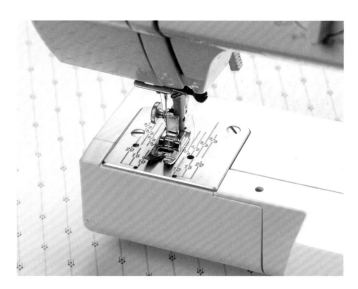

Sewing machines have marks for the seam allowance to the right of the presser foot. Many have only the number marked in inches, many only have the number marked in metric, and some have both. Older machines have been known to only have lines with no numbers, so to figure out which is which, place your needle in the center needle position, lower it about halfway, then take your seam gauge and measure the distance from the needle to the lines to determine what they represent. Refer to your machine's manual if you need help.

Choosing a Size

When deciding which size to make, it is important to consider a few things first. Ease—the distance between the finished garment and your body—is a very important consideration when selecting a size. Think about the style of the item, your personal taste, how you like to wear your clothing, and your style of living. The two dresses below have very different amounts of ease included in them. They are for the same size woman, but the one on the left has a fitted bodice and full skirt, while the one on the right is a loose-fitting dress.

You must determine for yourself what your own personal amount of ease is for every garment you make. Think about what is in your closet; which items are your favorites and why? If you like the way something fits, try to mimic that amount of ease in your sewing. After you take your body measurements, consult both the body size chart on the pattern envelope as well as the finished garment measurements to determine which size is best for your body and your personal preference of ease. From there, you can decide on a size and move forward with cutting out the pattern pieces and constructing the garment.

MEASURING YOUR BODY

There's nothing more disappointing than putting hours of work into sewing a garment, only to be unhappy with the way it fits. This is why it's so important to be honest about your real body measurements, and use real numbers as your guide. It is best to have someone help you with measurements, making sure that your tape measure is level, and verifying measurements in spots that you cannot see.

Take these measurements in your proper undergarments with very little else on, so the numbers are as accurate as possible. When taking measurements, be sure to use a fiberglass tape measure, which does not stretch. Pull the tape measure to fit snugly around your body, but not too tight. Stand as you would naturally without holding your breath. You want real measurements, not those taken in an unnatural state. Have a notepad on hand and write down your measurements as you go.

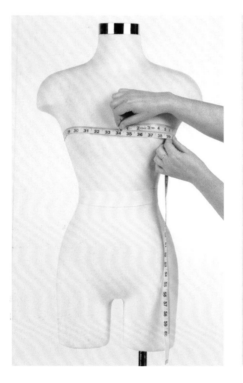  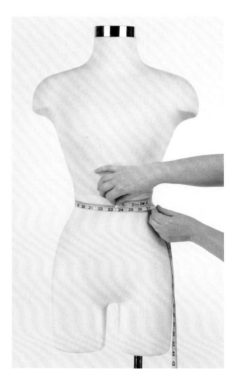

Bust

Pull the tape measure around the fullest part of your bust, keeping the tape measure level across your back.

Upper or High Bust

To measure your upper bust or high bust, place the tape measure across the widest part of your back, under your arms, and above your bust.

Natural Waist

When you bend to the side, you will crease at the smallest part of your body. This is your natural waist. Tie a string around your waist and mark the measurement on that string to use for future measurements.

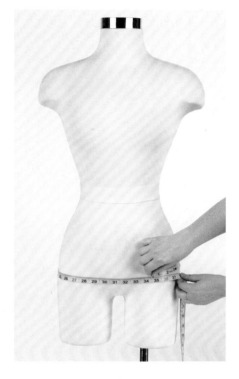 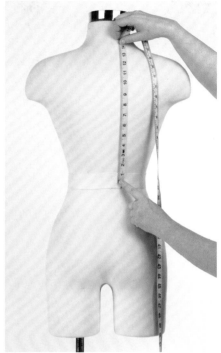 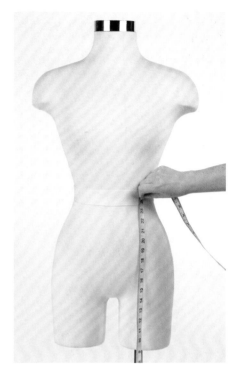

Hip

Your hip is the fullest part of your lower body, which is typically around 9" (22.9 cm) below your waist. If not, measure at the widest part. Note that the hip measurement on commercial sewing patterns is taken at that 9" (22.9 cm) mark, so if your measurement is higher or lower, write that down in your notes.

Back Neck to Waist

At the base of your neck is a bone that is more prominent than others. Measure the distance from that spot to your natural waist. This will indicate if you need to shorten or lengthen bodice pieces in future projects.

Natural Waist to Hem

If you have a length at which you prefer to wear skirts or dresses, measure from your waist to that spot and mark it down for future reference. Then you can quickly check to see how different a particular pattern is from your desired length.

Types of Fabric

For as many garments as there are in the world, there are nearly as many types of fabric, combinations, and content, with new developments being made every day. This is a guide to some of the basic types of fabric you will encounter in your sewing, but know that there are many more to learn about and explore.

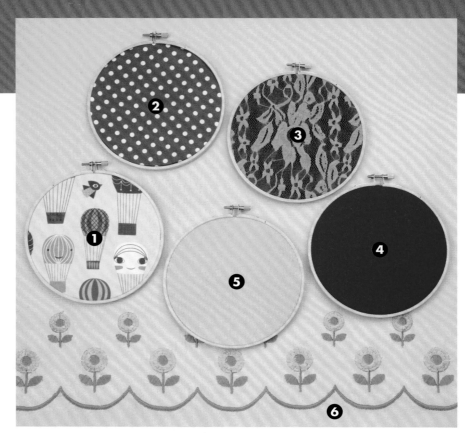

DIRECTIONAL PRINTS / QUILT-WEIGHT COTTON (1)

A print that is right-side up one way and upside down the other way is considered a directional print. Using a directional print will likely require more fabric, as all the elements need to be facing the same direction. This fabric is also a quilt-weight cotton—a medium-weight, 100% cotton that is often used for quilting, children's wear, and adult clothing because it is breathable and durable.

SILK (2)

Silks are both lovely to wear and challenging to work with due to their slippery nature. When sewing with silks, use pressing cloths to avoid making any marks on the fabric. Also use a silk machine needle and pins and mark as little as possible.

LACE (3)

Lace fabric is usually sheer, thus requiring some planning when using for garment construction. French seams hide all seam allowances, and underlining or lining the fabric provides coverage where the sheer lace does not.

WOOL (4)

Fine wool is the loveliest of fabrics in cold seasons and is nice to work with. Wool comes in a wide range of types, like boiled wool, wool flannel, and suiting. The weight and content blends depend on your project.

CORDUROY (5)

Fabrics that have a "nap" like corduroy are treated much like a directional print, in that there is a right and wrong direction to the nap and all pattern pieces need to be turned the same way in the cutting process. Typically, corduroy is 100% cotton, or, if it's a stretch version, a cotton blend.

BORDER PRINT (6)

A border print is a fabric with a print that faces the selvage, so it is used on the cross grain rather than on the length of grain. This embellished edge would need to be incorporated into the garment construction in the early planning stages, but it is always worth the extra work for the custom look that a border print can provide.

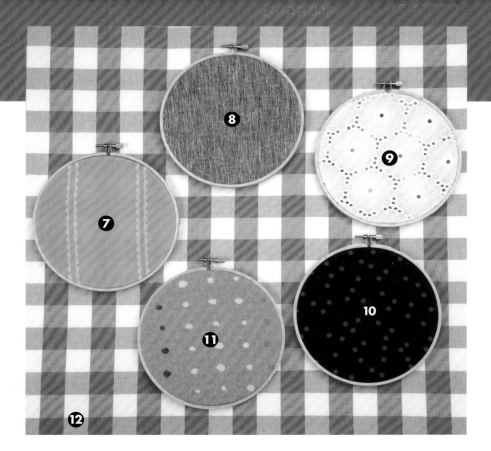

VOILE (7)

Voile for garment construction is a very thin cotton with a drape and feel much like silk, but without the shine. If you desire the fluidity of silk with a fabric that is easier to work with, voile is an excellent choice.

LINEN (8)

Linen is an elegant natural fiber choice that is made in a variety of weights. It is available in heavy jacket weight as well as lightweight handkerchief varieties, and the variance in the fibers provides interesting, unpredictable texture.

EYELET (9)

Much like lace, eyelet is woven to include open areas. Usually made in 100% cotton, eyelet provides the same appeal as lace, but is an easier fabric to work with.

DOUBLE GAUZE (10)

Gauze is a thin layer of loosely woven cotton. To make double gauze, two layers of gauze are stitched together in loose stitches all over the fabric. It is a very soft fabric that is great for summer dresses and children's wear.

KNIT (11)

Knit fabrics are not woven the way all these other fabrics are. The threads are knitted together, resulting in a fabric that stretches, like a T-shirt. Different needles, pins, and stretch-specific sewing patterns are required for working with this fabric.

SHIRTING (12)

Unlike fabrics with a printed design, shirting fabrics are woven with different colored threads to create the design. Most shirting fabrics are cotton or cotton and polyester blends and are often used to make men's button-down shirts.

Types of Interfacing

Interfacing is an extra layer of fabric that is sewn into or adhered inside your garment to give strength and body to elements in construction. It will appear in collars, facings, button plackets, and other spots in the garment that need a bit of support and shaping. Pattern instructions will request you to use either fusible or sew-in interfacing, depending on the situation and fabric type. There are many varieties of interfacing, from lightweight to heavy weight, as well as woven and nonwoven varieties. The weight of your interfacing should complement the weight of your fabric.

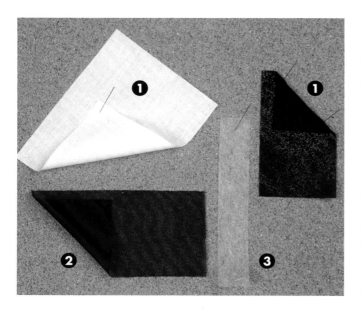

FUSIBLE INTERFACING

Fusible interfacing has glue on one or two sides that is melted onto your fabric when pressed with an iron. Always use a pressing cloth between your interfacing and iron as well as between your fabric and your ironing board to keep the adhesive off those surfaces.

Lightweight Woven Fusible Interfacing (1)

This is one of the most commonly used weights in garment construction. It is lightweight, so it is ideal for collars and facings, and it is woven, so it is actual fabric that will not disintegrate with washing and wearing. Because it is made of woven fabric, you must take the grainline into account when cutting just as you do with your pattern pieces on the garment fabric. It is available in both white and black for use with light and dark fabrics. Woven fusible interfacing also is available in medium- and heavy-weight options, for use with heavier fabric or when extra body is needed.

Knit Fusible Interfacing (2)

Perfect for knit, jersey, and other stretch fabrics, this interfacing is a lightweight knit that has some give and stretch. It also comes in both white and black to match with your fabric's color.

Fusible Tape (3)

Often used for ironing hems, this nonwoven fusible interfacing tape is fusible on both sides, so it can be placed between two fabrics to fuse them together. Fusible tape is often used for no-sew hems or to create a patch.

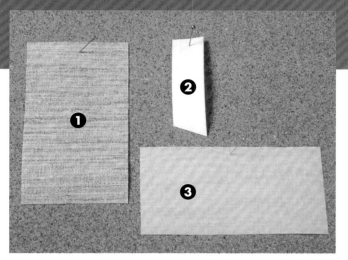

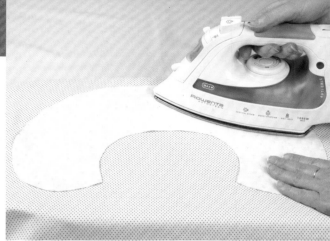

SEW-IN INTERFACING

Just like fusible interfacing, sew-in interfacing gives support to garment pieces, but it is sewn into place rather than ironed onto the fabric. Sew-in interfacing is best used in enclosed areas of construction, like inside a collar, in a men's tie, or between your fabric and lining.

Hair Canvas (1)

This sew-in interfacing is often found in jacket and coat tailoring to add stiffness and body. Sew-in interfacing is typically used in collars, cuffs, pocket flaps, and other locations that require extra support.

Belt Interfacing (2)

When making fabric-covered belts, inserting this stiff interfacing helps the inside of the belt hold its shape. Fold the fabric around the belt and cut it into whatever end shape you desire.

Lightweight Woven Sew-In Interfacing (3)

Exactly like the lightweight woven fusible version, this interfacing consists of a lightweight woven cotton fabric that provides body and strength to areas in garment construction like collars, pockets, cuffs, and facings. Place the pattern pieces with either grain, cross or lengthwise, when cutting out. This is also available in medium and heavyweight varieties, for when additional strength is needed.

HOW TO IRON FUSIBLE INTERFACING

Place a pressing cloth on your ironing board to protect it from the interfacing's adhesive. Place your fabric on the pressing cloth, wrong side up. Place your fusible interfacing onto the fabric, glue-side down. Place another pressing cloth down on top of your interfacing, to prevent your iron from sticking to the adhesive. Gently lay it down, careful not to move the pieces underneath out of place.

Using an iron set to the temperature instructed on the interfacing's instructions, place your iron onto your pressing cloth and hold in place. Using both hands to apply even pressure, move the iron in small circles for about 10 seconds for most types of interfacing. Pick up the iron and move to the next section of the interfacing, again being careful not to shift the pieces around. Do not move the iron back and forth, simply pick it up and set it back down.

After ironing the entire surface, peel back the pressing cloth and check to make sure the bond is permanent; otherwise, the interfacing will separate from the fabric as you wash and wear the item.

Preparing Fabric

To prevent unwanted shrinkage, color bleeding, and other shifts in the fabric, it is a smart idea to take the time to prepare your fabric prior to cutting out the pieces of your pattern. All fabric will change slightly after laundering, so there is no point in carefully measuring your body, making pattern adjustments, and sewing your entire garment together if after washing it is all going to shrink and no longer be the size it once was. To set yourself up for success, prewash your fabric and interfacing before you start cutting anything.

PREWASHING FABRIC

When prewashing your fabric, be sure to do so in a method appropriate for the type of fabric you are sewing with, taking into account the method you intend to use to care for your finished garment.

Woven cottons can be preshrunk in a washer and dryer to soften and remove the starch that is on the fabric from the manufacturing process. Linens also are well suited for washing using a traditional method. However, if you plan to use a cotton canvas or heavy-weight linen for a lined jacket and intend to dry clean after constructed, then you want to pretreat the fabric by dry cleaning it instead of machine washing it.

Silks should be washed by hand and then rolled in a thick towel to extract the water instead of wringing and wrinkling unnecessarily. Note that many silks lose their polish when washed and as a result are left with a more brushed finish. To avoid this, dry clean your fabric and the finished item instead of washing by hand.

Wool fabrics should also be pretreated with dry cleaning to prepare them for the same laundering when the garment is finished. If placed in a machine washer or dryer, wool will shrink terribly.

Knit fabrics, especially cotton knits, will shrink a great deal, sometimes as much as 25 percent of the original size. This makes it especially important to prewash all knit fabrics prior to cutting or else your garment will be 25 percent smaller than you had intended it to be.

When in doubt as to how to handle your fabric, consult the manufacturer of the fabric or the place of purchase.

PREWASHING INTERFACING

Because it is made of fabric, woven interfacing must also be prewashed to prevent shrinkage. If the interfacing is not preshrunk, it can create bumps on the surface of the garment as it shrinks. Be especially sensitive when washing fusible woven interfacing, as you want to prevent the glue from melting during the prewashing process.

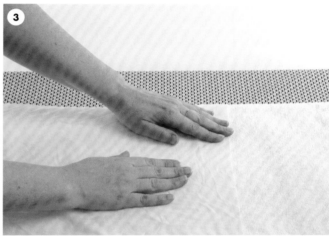

1. Soak the woven interfacing in lukewarm water without soap for about 15 minutes.

2. Pull the interfacing out of the soak and let it hang in your hands for a minute or two to let excess water drip off.

3. Lay the interfacing onto a thick towel on a flat surface that will not be damaged if it gets wet.

4. Roll the towel to extract the water from the interfacing into the towel.

5. Hang the interfacing overnight to finish drying. Once completely dry, proceed with cutting and sewing the interfacing.

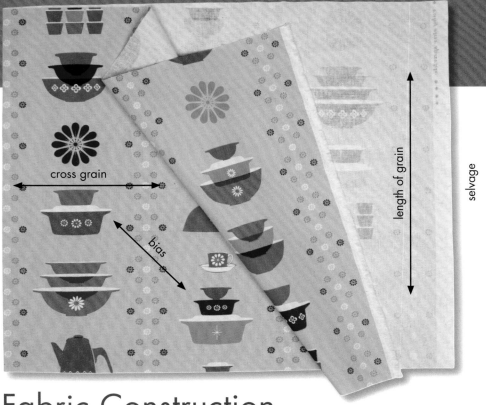

cross grain

bias

length of grain

selvage

Fabric Construction

It is important to understand how fabric is made in order to work with it properly. All fabric, whether it is a "stretch" fabric or not, does in fact stretch in certain directions and at an angle. In order for your project to be successful, the stretch of the fabric must go the correct way in accordance with the pattern pieces, or else the seams might ripple, warp, and stretch in unwanted ways. It also might not fit the intended wearer, because the stretch needs to go around the body as the pattern manufacturer designed.

Traditional woven fabric is made up of rows of threads going with the length of the fabric and rows of thread going across the fabric. The threads going with the length are the "length of grain" and are pulled tight in production. These threads have little to no stretch. The threads going across the fabric are the "cross grain" and they weave through the length of grain threads. These threads are not pulled as tight and offer a little stretch. As they reach each side, they loop back and continue to the other side. These finished edges are the "selvage" edges and do not fray. The 45-degree diagonal across the threads is the "bias," which has the most stretch in a woven fabric.

Cutting Layouts

All patterns come with a set of cutting layouts inside the envelope as part of the instruction sheet. Follow these layouts carefully, as they are critical for maximizing your fabric quantity. Each pattern company lays out all the pattern pieces required for each view that is offered in the pattern and determines how best to fit the pieces onto the fabric. This is how the quantity is determined on the back of the envelope.

Some sizes will have different layouts, as the pieces will fit differently when they are enlarged or reduced in size. Be sure to follow the layout for your view, size, and fabric width. It is a good practice to pin all the pieces for the project onto the fabric prior to cutting. This will ensure that enough fabric was bought, and you will not be left with a surprise at the end with too many pieces and not enough fabric.

There is also a cutting layout for interfacing, if required for your project, as well as any contrasting fabrics. Look to the layout code to inform you as to which elements are the right side of the fabric, the wrong side of the fabric, contrasting fabrics, or interfacing and follow them closely.

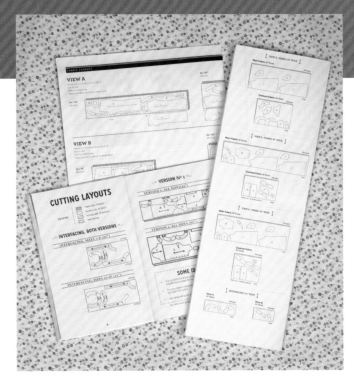

Pinning and Cutting

A well-made garment consists of a series of well-executed steps. One of the first permanent steps is pinning and cutting out your fabric. Take time to carefully lay out each piece onto the fabric and pin and cut with care.

PLACING PIECES ON GRAIN

Because fabric will stretch more in certain directions than others, it is important that each piece is cut in accordance with how the pattern designer intended, or else the elements of the garment will not go together well. The little bit of stretch that is in the "cross grain" of the fabric should go around the body and not down the body. To ensure this, every pattern piece has a "place on grain" line drawn on it, known as the "grainline."

This "grainline" needs to be parallel to your selvage edges at all times. If it is not and the cross grain stretch has been turned to be going down the body, it will be very difficult to wear the garment, especially if it is fitted.

The pattern designer is counting on that little bit of stretch to make the item wearable. Likewise, if the pattern pieces are turned on a diagonal and the pattern is aligned with the "bias" stretch, the pattern pieces will warp and stretch a lot more than intended. Follow these steps to ensure the pattern pieces are "on grain" on the fabric.

Some garments account in the pattern making process for them to be made on the "cross grain" or "on bias" and are sized accordingly. You cannot just move the pattern pieces to the cross grain or bias without any changes in the pattern making and fitting, so take time to read how the elements are meant to go together.

(continued)

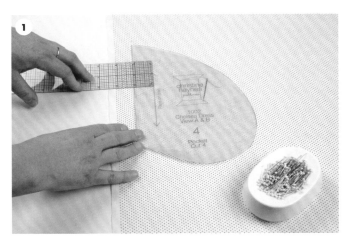

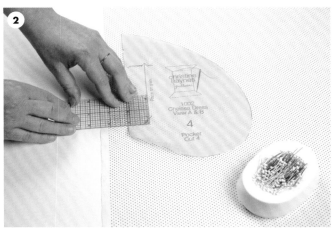

1. Using a clear ruler, measure the distance from the top edge of the grainline to the selvage edge. Make note of the distance and pin in place.

2. Repeat that process at the bottom edge of the grainline, moving the pattern piece until the distance is equal to the previous measurement. Pin in place.

3. Continue by pinning the rest of the edges of the piece to the fabric.

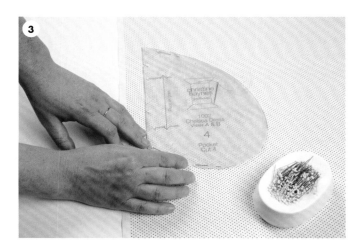

PINNING TIPS

Pinning the pattern pieces down seems like an easy step, but it takes some getting used to. It is best to do all of the pinning from the top of the fabric, refraining from putting part of your hand under the fabric. This only shifts the pattern piece around, making the pinning less precise.

Place the pattern piece "on grain" or on the fold of the fabric. Insert the pin into the fabric and through all the layers until you have hit the surface underneath. Gently raise the point of the pin up, going through all the layers of the fabric back to the top.

Keep both hands on the fabric, supporting it in place. Pin with the length of the pin parallel to the edge of the pattern piece, thus flattening more of the edge as you go around each piece.

Move around the pattern piece, placing the pins end to end, with enough coverage to prevent your scissors from slipping under the pattern piece. The end result is to have a piece of fabric the exact same size as the pattern piece, so you want to prevent accidently cutting the piece smaller than desired. Also be sure to keep the pin heads and tips entirely contained inside the pattern piece, so you will not hit them with the scissors while cutting.

CUTTING TIPS

Using your sharp fabric scissors, place the lower blade flat on the cutting surface and support the fabric with the other hand. It is okay to lift the fabric a little, but refrain from raising it more than the height of the scissor blade.

While cutting, be aware if the cutting is easier when cutting on the right side of the pattern piece or the left. Many sewers are more precise on one side or the other. Cut as close as you can to the pattern paper without actually cutting it.

Slowly and gently, work around the pattern piece, being extra careful on curves. Use medium-size cuts for the most accuracy.

Once the pattern pieces are cut, keep them pinned until all the markings are done. Set each piece aside as you cut and move on to the next piece.

If the amount of fabric on the edge around the pattern piece is small, cutting it exactly can be difficult. The best solution for a precise cut is to support the little border of fabric with the hand opposite your cutting hand. Hold the scissors and cut along the edge while keeping the extra fabric secure with the other hand. This will provide the cleanest cut.

Special Fabric Layouts

Certain fabrics come with inherent challenges, such as stripes, plaids, and directional prints. If you want designs to match at side seams and other critical points in the garment, you must lay the pieces onto the fabric correctly. Shifting the pattern pieces around on the fabric to align markings often requires more fabric than the suggested allotment on the back of the pattern envelope.

CUTTING STRIPES

Horizontal stripes should go around the body in a straight level line, and should match at side seams. To accomplish this, pay close attention to the following details.

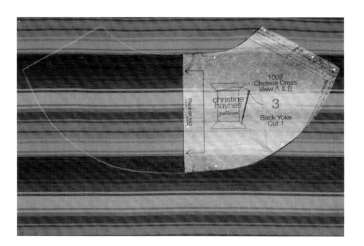

Cutting Stripes on the Fold

When cutting a piece on the fold, to make sure that the stripes are level across the piece, cut it in one layer instead of two. Open the folded edge of the fabric and press it flat. Place your pattern piece on grain and, with a water-soluble pencil, draw around the piece including marking the line that would have been the fold. Unpin the pattern piece, flip it for a mirror image of the marked half, and lay the "place on fold" edge along the newly drawn fold line. Pin in place, keeping it on grain, so the stripes on the mirror image side are in the same spot as the other side. Cut around the entire piece.

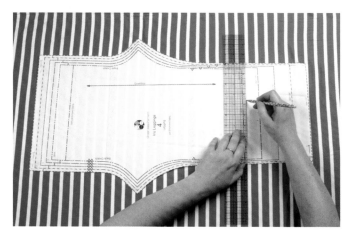

Cutting Stripes on a Side Seam

To ensure that stripes line up on side seams, use a pencil and ruler to mark the placement of the stripes on your pattern piece. Placing a dot or notch on the top or bottom of a stripe can be helpful, as the notch becomes an anchor on which to start the second matching piece. Use the lines on the pattern piece as a guide for the next piece. When pinning them together, line up and pin at each stripe and sew with caution, keeping the stripes lined up.

CUTTING PLAIDS

Just as with stripes, the main "stripe" of the plaid can be used as a starting point for all the markings. And, as with all prints where you need to align elements, be sure to buy additional fabric so you can move the pattern pieces around to land where you desire.

Cutting Plaids on a Side Seam

As with stripes, plaids need to be marked on the pattern piece and used as a guide for other pieces to follow. Insert pins into a key motif or element on the pattern and draw the plaid onto the pattern piece using a pencil and ruler. Cut each piece one at a time, never with layers of the fabric together, and line up the guide you drew onto the pattern piece to mirror the print on the seams that intersect with each other.

For cutting a piece on the fold, follow the same technique for cutting a stripe on the fold (opposite).

DIRECTIONAL PRINTS

Many prints have imagery that is upright in one direction and upside down in the other. Take care to lay out all the pieces of the garment in the correct direction.

Pattern companies print the text on all the pattern pieces with the pattern in the upright direction. Some pattern companies indicate the waist seam or the hem, but many do not, so keep in mind where each piece goes in the garment in relation to your body and the print to make sure the print is consistent from piece to piece.

CUTTING WITH NAP

Fabrics like corduroy, velvet, and velour have a texture called "nap" that is a brushed "pile" on the face of the fabric. The nap is smooth in one direction and rough in the opposite direction. Typically, the smooth side of the nap on these fabrics goes down the body so when light hits it, it reflects off nicely and does not absorb it into the fabric.

Just like with directional prints, be sure to lay out your pattern pieces with the nap running down the pattern pieces as they would down the body, from head to toe.

Marking Fabric

Now that you have cut your fabric, all the dots, circles, lines, and dashes that the pattern designer carefully marked on the pattern piece must be transferred to your pieces. There are a variety of ways to do this, but my preferred method is to use marking tools. All marking tools should be tested on a scrap of fabric to ensure they will be removed from the fabric when washed or left out in the air. It is also important to have a delicate, conservative hand when marking, as it is easy to overdo the marking process.

Each type of marking tool leaves a different size mark. These lines might all look the same, but each type is different from the rest.

CHALK TRIANGLE WEDGE (1)

The chalk wedge comes in a variety of shapes, the most common being the triangle. These chalks are rarely water soluble and it is best to test them prior to pressing with a hot iron, as the heat can set the chalk in place. These wedges can produce a fine line when the edges are brand new and sharp, but they will dull and become wider quickly with use. These are best for big, broad strokes on muslins and other areas that do not need precision.

CHALK PENCILS (2)

Because these can be sharpened until gone, the chalk pencil is a finer point for details like darts, pleats, pivoting, and other fine details. If the chalk pencils are water soluble, these are also perfect for marking details like collar pivots and buttonholes on the outside of your fabric, as it will wash out of most fabrics.

MARKING PENS (3)

For an even more precise line, use an air- or water-soluble marking pen. These are only well suited for lighter colors because the marker shows up in a dark value and will blend in with darker fabrics. As always, be sure to test on a scrap to make sure the pen will not ruin the fabric.

Cutting Notches

Notches are triangle shapes on the cut edges of the pattern pieces. Most pieces will have one or more notches, which are there to tell you where the elements of the pattern line up. Two notches on a pattern piece usually means that the piece falls on the back of the body, while one notch on a pattern piece usually means that the piece falls on the front of the body.

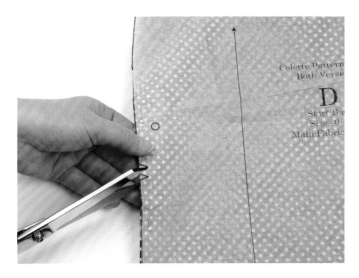

When cutting notches, make sure your pattern piece is pinned to the fabric with all edges lining up. Ideally, this step would be done prior to unpinning the pattern piece from the fabric.

Using only the tips of your scissors, cut the notches into the fabric. Do not cut beyond the markings as you might cut beyond the allotted seam allowance. If the notch is marked both into and outside the cutting line, double check that you have enough room in the seam allowance for the notch to go into the fabric. If not, cut around the notches while cutting the piece out, leaving a triangle of fabric sticking out from the side of the cutting edge.

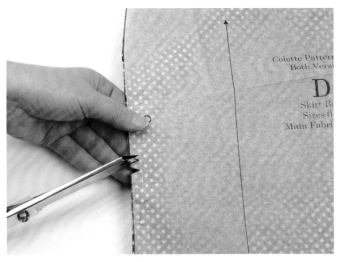

Once all your notches and other marks have been made, unpin the pattern piece and use those markings to properly align the elements and pieces.

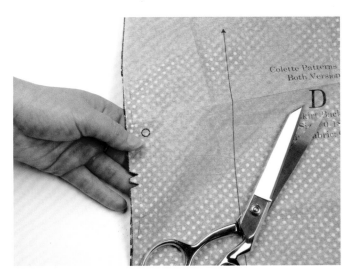

Anatomy of a Garment

Rolled collar (1)	Double fold sleeve hem (6)
Understitching (2)	Bust darts (7)
Buttonholes (3)	Knife pleats (8)
Flat buttons (4)	In-seam pockets (9)
Set-in sleeves (5)	Hand stitched hem (10)

Clipping curves (1)	Gathering (6)
Understitching (2)	In-seam pockets (7)
Topstitching (3)	Seam finishing (8)
Princess seams (4)	Double fold dress hem (9)
Bias binding sleeveless finishing (5)	

Flat collar (1)	Bust darts (6)
Pivoting (2)	Buttonholes (7)
Facings (3)	Shank buttons (8)
Understitching (4)	Release pleats (9)
Double fold sleeve hem (5)	Double fold shirt hem (10)

Seam grading (1)	Buttonhole (5)
Clipping curves (2)	Flat button (6)
Understitching (3)	Fly zipper (7)
Topstitching (4)	Seam finishing (8)

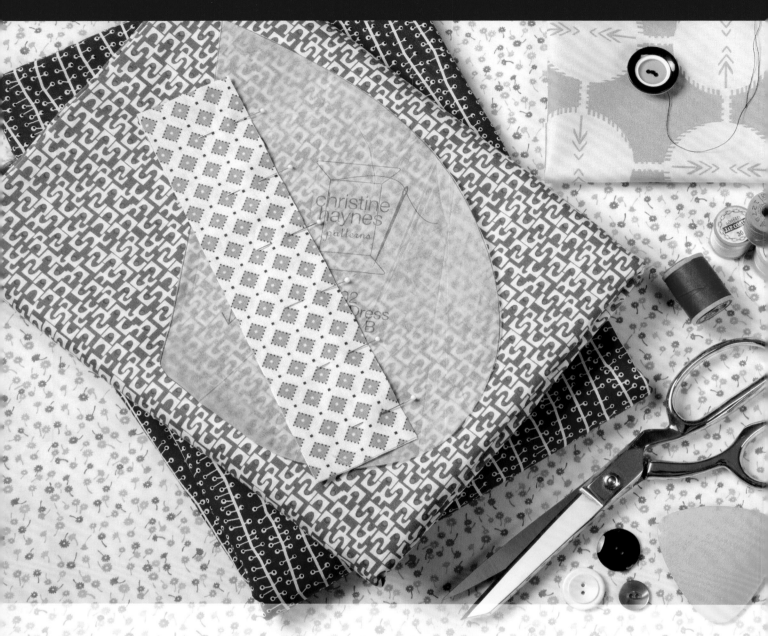

CONSTRUCTION BASICS

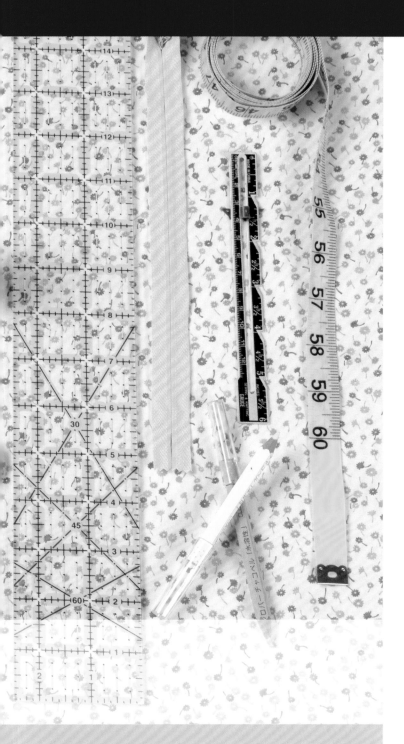

ow that you've selected the fabric, measured the body, and cut the pattern pieces, it is time to begin the basic construction of the garment. In this chapter I will discuss the many different ways to sew a seam, show you how to hand sew certain elements, and provide some tips for tackling important elements such as buttons and zippers. There is a lot of information in this chapter, so take some time to review each section carefully.

Sewing Machine Stitches

Though most sewing machines come with anywhere from one to hundreds of stitch choices, the reality is that you only need a handful of stitches to create quality garments. The most basic stitches—straight stitch, zigzag stitch, and 3-step zigzag—are the most common stitches used in all garment construction; you will use these stitches over and over again. In this section, I will cover how to sew all the basic stitches you will encounter in your future garments.

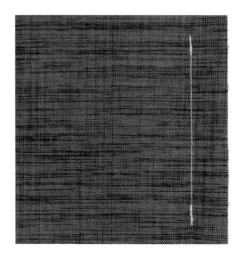

HOW TO SEW A STRAIGHT STITCH SEAM WITH BACKSTITCH

The most basic construction stitch is also the one most often used in all projects: the straight stitch seam. More often than not, you will be sewing with this stitch, so it is important to understand what a good stitch looks like. A straight stitch with proper tension consists of clean, even, straight dashes with no puckering in the fabric or bumps in the stitch. Follow these steps for a perfect stitch every time.

For medium-weight fabrics, a typical stitch length is 2.5, 2.0 for lighter fabrics, and up to 3.0 for heavier fabrics. Consult your machine's manual for the manufacturer's suggestion on the setting for ideal stitch length on your specific machine.

1. Using the proper pins for your fabric type, insert the pins perpendicular to your seam edge. Place the pins with the head of the pin off to the right of the fabric so they are easy to remove when sewing. For basic stitching, placing them approximately 1" (2.5 cm) apart is adequate, but for many other situations like sewing gathering, curves, or corners, use more pins to hold everything in place while sewing.

2. Insert the fabric into the sewing machine so that the fabric is visible inside the presser foot and on top of the feed. Align the right side of the fabric with the project's seam allowance. Lower the presser foot onto the fabric.

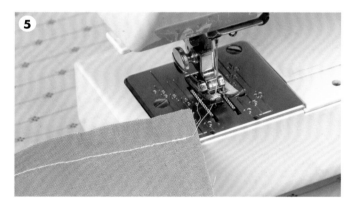

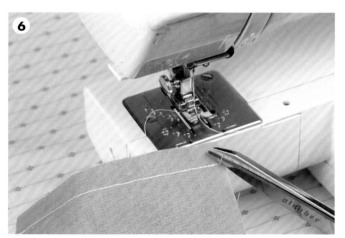

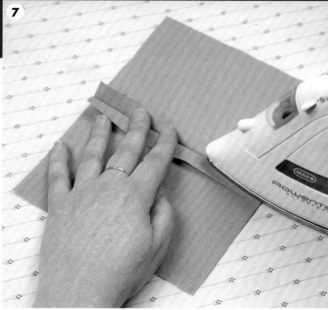

3. For a permanent seam, start with a backstitch. Sew forward about three stitches. Stop, select the reverse button on the machine, and return to your starting point, sewing the straight stitch backward. Continue sewing the seam, pulling out the pins as you approach them.

4. Continue to the end of your seam and stop just short of the end of the fabric. Finish with a backstitch by selecting the reverse button and sewing backward about three stitches. Unselect the reverse button and sew straight, finishing at the end of the fabric.

5. For electronic machines, the machine will finish the stitch for you and return the needle to the upright position. For manual machines, turn the hand wheel toward you until the needle is in the upmost position. Pull the fabric out of the machine, bringing a few inches of thread with it.

6. Clip the threads from the seam close to your fabric. The backstitching will prevent the stitching from coming undone. Trim the threads at the start of the seam as well. Pull the threads from the bobbin and needle so they are a few inches long, push them under the presser foot, and leave them hanging behind the machine so they are ready for your next stitch.

7. Press your seam according to the project step instructions and fabric type.

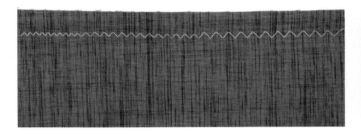

ZIGZAG STITCH

A zigzag stitch is a stitch that makes the letter Z when sewn and is one single stitch from point to point. A zigzag stitch will provide seam finishing or stretch when sewn into elastic, and can be used for decoration as well. The stitch can be used in any combination of wide, narrow, short, and long to get the stitch you desire. See the section on seam finishing to learn how to use this stitch in a variety of ways to finish the insides of your garments.

3-STEP ZIGZAG STITCH

A 3-step zigzag stitch is exactly like a regular zigzag stitch, except instead of having only one stitch from point to point, a 3-step zigzag sews three stitches from point to point. This can provide a zigzag stitch that lays flat, especially in finer fabrics, where a regular zigzag stitch has a tendency to bunch up the fabric. Later in this chapter, there are many seam finishing options using this stitch.

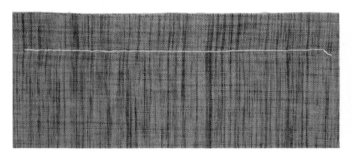

BASTING STITCH

A baste stitch is a straight stitch that has a longer stitch length and is used to hold the fabric together temporarily. This stitch is not backstitched, as it is most often removed after a permanent straight stitch is sewn in its place. The baste stitch is used later in the book for gathering, for setting sleeves, and in most zipper insertions. To achieve a baste stitch, set up your machine for a regular straight stitch and turn the length up to at least 4.0.

STAY STITCH

A stay stitch is a stitch that is sewn into a curve to lock the threads of the garment in place and prevent it from stretching out of shape when handled during the construction process. Most often found on necklines, this stitch lands just inside the project's seam allowance and is left in place. It is not removed like a baste stitch, as it should be as tight as a regular straight stitch to ensure the threads of the garment are held in place.

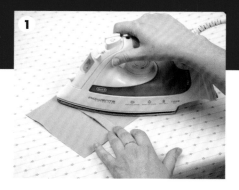

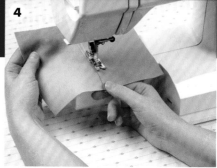

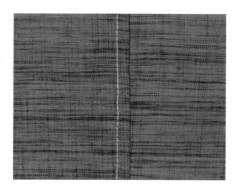

HOW TO SEW UNDERSTITCHING

Understitching is when you sew the facing of a seam to the seam allowance. This keeps the facing inside the garment, preventing it from coming up to the right side. Understitching is most often used on necklines. In that instance, you would sew the neckline facing to the neckline, press the seam allowance toward the facing, then stitch the facing to the seam allowance. Follow these steps to use this technique on your next project.

1. Sew the facing to the garment. Press the seam allowance toward the facing.

2. Insert the piece into the sewing machine with the facing and seam allowance on the same side. Pin in place if necessary.

3. Using a regular straight stitch, sew just to the side of the seam on the facing, stitching through the seam allowance underneath.

4. Continue around the entire piece, staying just to the side of the seam.

5. Trim, clip, notch, or grade the seam allowance depending on the shape and location of the seam.

6. Press the seam flat. The stitching should remain on the inside, the seam should be centered, and the front of the garment should be free of all stitching.

TOPSTITCHING

Any decorative or functional stitch that can be seen on the outside of the finished garment is considered topstitching. In decorative situations, this would be the stitching around the edges of a Peter Pan collar or around pockets on pants. Topstitching may be used for functional purposes, too, as when you sew a hem with exposed stitching, on a sleeve or skirt hem, or if you were sewing bias binding to a neck. These are all "topstitched" and the thread is exposed on the outside. You'll find tutorials on all of these examples later in the book.

Hand Sewing Stitches

No matter how much can be done with a sewing machine, there are many reasons to resort to sewing certain elements by hand. In fact, in some instances, it is even preferred for a nicer, more couture finish. Use this sampler to familiarize yourself with all the basic hand stitches.

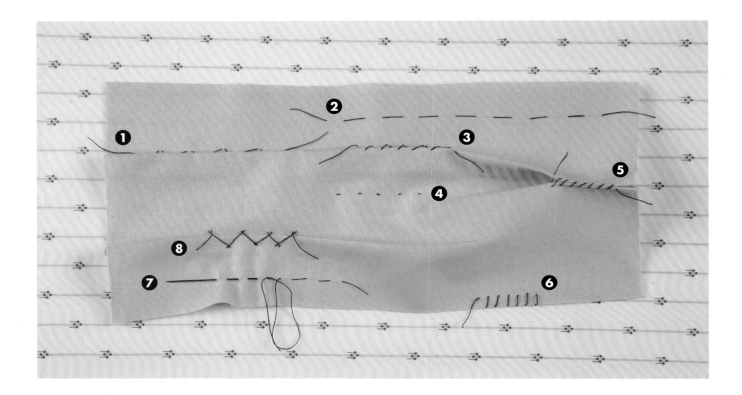

SLIPSTITCH (1)

This is the most common hand sewing stitch for hemming. The stitch will leave tiny dots on the right side of the garment and if done well, is nearly just as invisible on the wrong side. Start this stitch at the top fold of a hem, then catch the inside of the folded piece. Take the needle up slightly to the back side of the finished garment and put the needle through, only catching the tiniest amount. Repeat this, keeping the stitches evenly spread out so the tiny dots on the right side are even and consistent.

BASTING STITCH (2)

Just like machine basting, this is a temporary stitch that holds things together for a limited time. Basting by hand can be surprisingly fast and is great for fabrics that are too fragile to run through the machine over and over. This can be used in place of almost all machine basting, such as when working with set-in sleeves. These stitches should be evenly distributed and short to medium in length, around ¼–½" (6 mm–1.3 cm) each. Load a few stitches onto the needle and pull through in one motion.

HEMMING STITCH (3)

The end result on the right side of the fabric of the hemming stitch is identical to a slipstitch, but the hemming stitch is not invisible on the inside. Instead of hiding the stitching between the layers of the fabric, the hemming stitch is sewn through the face of the hem on the inside, then passed through to the right side of the garment with a tiny dot, and passed back through the hem.

PRICKSTITCH (4)

A prickstitch is most often used for hand sewing in zippers, and the thread length between the stitches is visible on the underside. Use long stitches on the underside and very short stitches on the right side. If made with matching thread, these right side stitches are nearly invisible.

WHIPSTITCH (5)

To create a whipstitch, simply insert the needle into finished or folded edges, catching a minimal amount of threads. There are a lot of basic reasons to use a whipstitch, and depending on the circumstance, the length will vary. Use this to secure a zipper at the end of the tape, to secure lining on the interior of a garment, and for many other practical uses.

OVERCAST STITCH (6)

To finish seam allowance by hand instead of with a zigzag or other machine stitch, an overcast stitch can be sewn along the edge of the fabric. This stitch is wrapped around the edge of the fabric and should be tighter or looser, depending on how much the fabric ravels.

RUNNING STITCH (7)

A running stitch looks like a baste stitch but they are shorter in length and sometimes left in permanently. Often used for mending and gathering, these stitches also are loaded onto the needle a few at a time, then pulled through at once.

FLAT CATCHSTITCH (8)

A flat catchstitch is a strong way to attach two fabrics to each other, making it ideal for hemming heavier fabrics like wool or canvas. As with the other hemming stitches, only evenly spaced tiny dots should be visible on the right side, while on the inside the thread is passed through the hem with a deep stitch, making a much more secure hem.

How to Use a Seam Ripper

The reality is, if you are sewing, you will need to pull out stitches from time to time. Sometimes this is planned for, such as when sewing in a zipper; other times it is because you made a mistake and need to remove stitches and re-sew. Either way, get comfortable using a seam ripper, because it is a very handy tool.

1. Insert the tip of the seam ripper under a thread and slide the thread to the U-shaped bevel. Gently cut the thread with the ripper. If it doesn't cut with ease, you might need a new, sharper seam ripper. Continue down the seam and cut the thread every few stitches.

2. On the front of the fabric, pull on the threads that you cut in step 1.

3. On the back of the fabric, pull on the thread and pull it out in one big piece. If the thread is resisting removal on either side of the fabric, be gentle because you do not want to tear or warp the threads of the fabric. Once all the thread is removed, press the fabric and try your stitch again.

How to Sew with Buttons

I love picking out buttons for my projects, as it can really change the look and feel of a garment once buttons have been added. Learning how to sew buttonholes and attaching buttons seems like the most basic of tasks, but there are right and wrong ways to do it. Follow these steps for making buttonholes and for attaching buttons with confidence.

MACHINE BUTTONHOLES

There is no one way that sewing machines make buttonholes, so please take some time to read the manual for your sewing machine make and model to learn how your individual machine works. A few general tips for creating buttonholes follow, which apply no matter what type of machine you own.

Marking Buttonholes

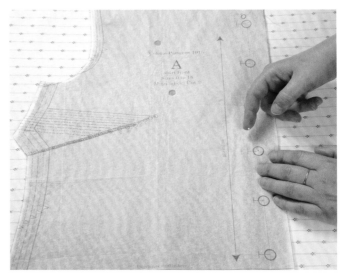

Follow the markings on the pattern you are using and transfer the marks to the fabric. The key element is the central dot for the button placement. This is your starting point and the center of the buttonhole. Consult the pattern to ensure you make the correct size holes and to confirm that they are the proper distance apart. For stability, most patterns will call for interfacing wherever a buttonhole is to be made. This helps keep the fabric firm and prevents warping and sagging.

To mark the dot placement on the fabric, insert a pin into the buttonhole mark on the pattern. Peel back the pattern and use a water-soluble marking tool to transfer the dot to the fabric.

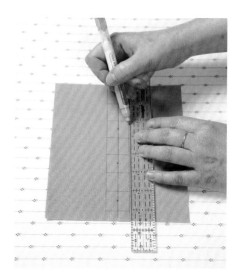
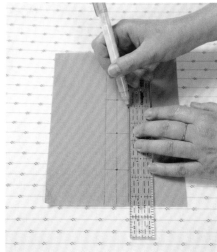
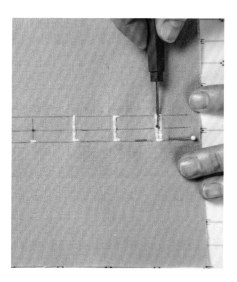

VERTICAL BUTTONHOLES

For vertical buttonholes, draw a line down the center of the buttonhole line. This is all done on the right side of the garment, so be sure to test your marking tool to ensure it will be removable afterward. Draw lines on either side of the buttonhole to mark the placket width. Then draw lines above and below the dot for the center of the button to indicate where the buttonhole will begin and end. In looking at this image, the buttonhole will be centered on the dot, starting and stopping at the lines above and below it.

HORIZONTAL BUTTONHOLES

The markings for horizontal buttonholes are quite similar to those for vertical buttonholes, but the buttonhole will be made from side to side, instead of from top to bottom, with the dot in the center. Draw the dot for the button placement first, and then draw the vertical line connecting them. Draw the outer lines to the right and left of the center line, indicating the width of the buttonhole, and lastly draw the line from side to side, for the horizontal buttonhole.

Some machines have a one-step buttonhole, while others have four-step and five-step buttonholes. Additionally, some machines start at the bottom and go up one side,

while others start at the top and come down first. They all do the same thing in the end, which is to form a bottom bar tack, a top bar tack, and two rows of tight zigzag stitching in between. This hole should be only slightly larger than the button fitting through it, and should suit the pattern you are using.

CUTTING A BUTTONHOLE

To cut open the buttonhole, you may use one of the buttonhole cutters available commercially or you may use a seam ripper. Commercial buttonhole cutters look like a chisel and cut buttonholes in one motion using a block of wood underneath. When using the seam ripper to cut buttonholes, insert a pin into the opposite end of the hole from where you are starting. Cut the fabric with the seam ripper, stopping just prior to the pin. Remove the pin, rotate the fabric, and cut any remaining threads. Remember to be careful with any task where you are permanently cutting through the fabric, as this cannot be undone.

How to Sew on Buttons

In sewing classes, I always hear students say, "I don't even know how to sew on a button!" This is not as easy as it seems and there are many ways in which to sew on a button. In this section, I will demonstrate four different methods for attaching buttons to your next project.

ATTACHING A FLAT BUTTON

A flat button is one that has either two or four holes through the button, and has a flat back. This button is attached by passing threads through the face of the button to the back and again to the front.

1

2

3

4

5

6

1. Refer to your pattern and use a water-soluble marking tool to mark the button's placement on the right side of the fabric.

2. Thread a needle and pass the needle through the dot you made in step 1. Do not knot the thread.

3. Pull the needle through the fabric, leaving behind a tail of thread.

4. Pass back through the dot with the needle and feed the needle through the loop of thread to knot.

5. Pull both ends of the thread to tighten and clip the thread at the knot.

6. Place the button on the needle, passing the needle through one of the holes.

7

8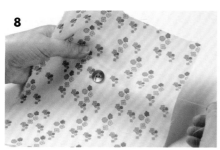

9

10

11

12

13

14

15

7. Feed the needle through the other hole on the face of the button. Insert the needle into the fabric at the starting spot, passing the needle to the back side of the fabric.

8. Pull the thread tight from the back of the fabric.

9. Bring the needle back up through the first hole to the right side of the fabric.

10. Insert the needle into the second hole, passing through to the back side again. Go through the button a couple of times until the button is secure.

11. Insert the needle from the back into the front, but not through the buttonhole. Rather, insert the needle into the fabric at the base of the button threads.

12. Bring the needle up to the right side of the fabric under the button near the threads.

13. Pass the needle through the fabric under the button, leaving a loop of thread.

14. Insert the needle through the loop of thread and pull tight to knot. Pull both ends of the thread to secure.

15. Clip the thread close to the knot under the button. This method hides all the knotting under the button and leaves the underside clean with just a few stitches.

ATTACHING A SHANK BUTTON

A shank button is flat on the top and has a loop of metal or plastic on the back side of the button that is used for securing it to the garment. Unlike a flat button, the thread does not pass through the button, and the shank provides a gap between the fabric and button, making this a great choice for thicker fabrics, jackets, and coats.

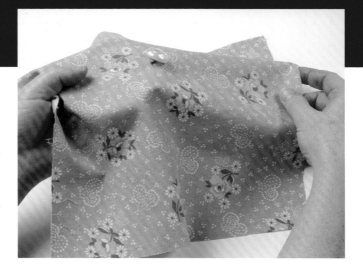

1

2

3

4

1. Refer to your pattern and use a water-soluble marking tool to mark the button's placement on the right side of the fabric.

2. Thread the needle and pass the needle through the fabric at the spot marked in step 1, leaving a tail of thread. Do not knot the thread. Instead, pass the needle through the fabric a second time and insert the needle through the loop of thread, knotting it in place.

3. Pull both ends of the thread tight to secure the knot.

4. Cut the thread tail at the knot.

5

6

8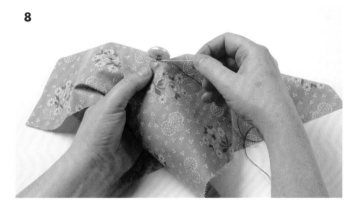

7

9

5. Feed the needle through the shank loop on the back of the button.

6. Insert the needle into the fabric at the starting point, passing through to the back of the fabric.

7. Insert the needle into the fabric on the back side, and pass it through to the front, going through the shank loop. Repeat a couple of times until the button is secure.

8. Feed the needle through the fabric under the button near the base of the shank. Do not pull the thread tight; instead, leave a loop of thread at the base.

9. Insert the needle through the loop of thread to knot. Pull both threads tight to secure, and clip the thread at the base.

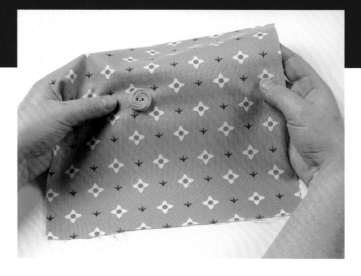

ATTACHING A FLAT BUTTON WITH A SHANK

If you'd like a flat button for a project that is made with thick fabric and need the extra lift under the button, you can create a thread shank. As you sew on the button, stitch over a toothpick or thick needle to extend the stitches. Then remove the item, lift up the button, and wind the thread around the extended stitches in the gap between the button and the fabric.

1

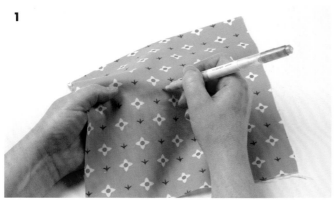

2

3

4

1. Refer to your pattern and mark the button placement on the right side of your fabric using a water-soluble marking tool.

2. Thread the needle and pass the needle through the mark made in step 1. Leave thread tails behind and do not knot the thread end.

3. Pass through a second time, then feed the needle through the loop of thread to create a knot.

4. Pull both ends of the thread to tighten the knot and secure the threads. Cut off the thread tail at the knot.

5

6

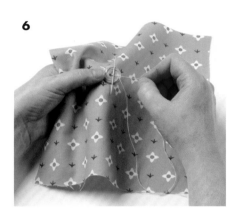

7

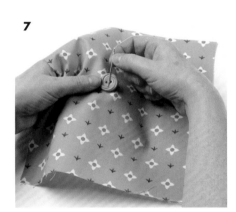

8

9

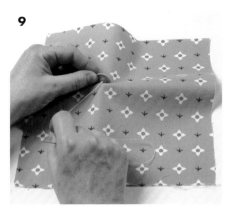

10

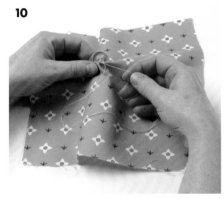

11

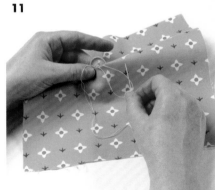

5. Put the button on the needle and pull the needle through. Rest the button on a flat surface.

6. Lay a large needle or toothpick on the face of the button between the holes. Insert the needle into the second hole and through the fabric at the starting point underneath. Trap the toothpick under the thread on the face of the button. Run the needle from the front of the button to the back a few more times, securing the button to the fabric. Do not pull the threads too tight while doing this step.

7. Simply pull out the toothpick to remove it.

8. Lift up the button to see the gap created underneath. At the base of the button threads, insert the needle from the back to the front of the fabric.

9. Tightly wind the thread from the needle around the threads under the button to create the shank.

10. Pass the needle through the thread shank at the base of the thread where it meets the fabric. Do not pull it tight; instead, leave a loop of thread.

11. Insert the needle through the loop to form a knot. Pull the threads tight to secure. Clip the threads.

ATTACHING A REINFORCED BUTTON WITH AN UNDER BUTTON

For areas in garments that need additional reinforcement and security, a button can be sewn to the inside of the garment opposite the outer button. This provides an added level of strength and works especially well for outerwear. Essentially you are sewing two buttons at once, through the eyes of the buttons. This is best done with two flat buttons with the same number of holes through them, and with an inside button that is much smaller than the outer button.

1

3

2

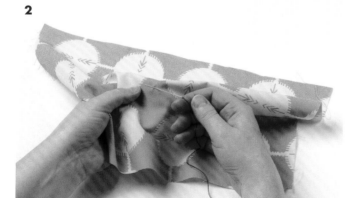

1. Use a water-soluble marking tool to mark the button placement on the right side of the fabric. Use the pattern's instructions as a guide.

2. Thread a needle and feed it through the spot marked in step 1. Do not pull the threads all the way through, and do not tie a knot at the end.

3. Feed the needle through a second time and pass the needle through the loop of thread to form a knot.

4

7

5

7

6

4. Pull both ends of the thread to tighten and secure the knot. Clip off the thread tail at the knot.

5. Place the outer button on the needle. Insert the needle through the other eye of the outer button, through the fabric at the base of the threads.

6. Feed the smaller inner button onto the needle on the back of the fabric. Insert the needle through the other eye of the small button, passing through the eye of the larger button on the other side. Pull the threads firmly so both buttons are tight against the fabric and each other.

7. Repeat step 6 by passing the needle through the eye of the large button into the eye of the smaller button, and back to the front of the fabric. Repeat a few times until both buttons are secure. On the final pass back to the front, pull the needle through to under the large button. Thread the needle through the fabric under the large button, leaving a loop of thread. Feed the needle through the thread loop and pull to knot. Pull threads to tighten and cut off at the knot.

6

How to Sew with Zippers

The other main closure you will find in commercial patterns is zippers. Some zipper insertions are lengthy, some are quick and easy, but all require a certain series of steps in order to work properly. In this section, I will show you how to use the most common types: the centered or "regular" zipper, an invisible zipper, a lapped regular zipper, and a fly-front zipper. Each has a very different approach.

As with buttons, all zipper insertions benefit from interfacing strengthening. But unlike with buttons, few patterns will actually explain that you should do this before sewing the zipper into the garment. For regular centered zippers, invisible zippers, and lapped zippers, cut a piece of lightweight fusible interfacing 1" (2.5 cm) wide and the length of the zipper, and press it to the wrong side of the zipper seam, so that when the zipper is being sewn, it is sewn through this interfacing. This will give the zipper much more strength and stability.

HOW TO SEW A CENTERED ZIPPER

A centered zipper is the most common type of zipper insertion. It is done with a regular zipper down the center of a seam and is found on nearly every type of sewn object in the world. It is worth practicing and getting good at, as you will encounter it again and again in patterns.

1. Refer to the pattern and mark the end of the zipper onto the fabric accordingly. Sew a baste stitch from the top of the seam to this mark, using the seam allowance indicated for the project you are sewing. When you hit the mark, switch to a regular stitch. Sew a backstitch and continue to sew to the other end of the seam.

2. Press this seam open. Transfer the mark for the zipper's end onto the other side of the seam allowance so you can see it when the seam is pressed open.

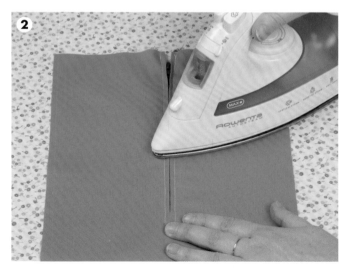

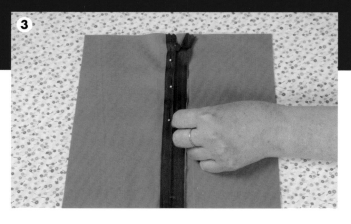

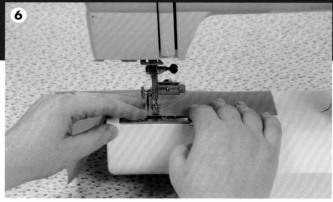

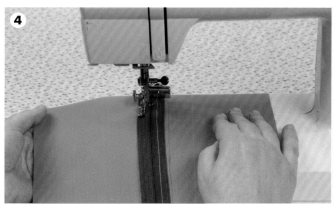

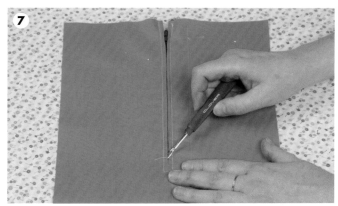

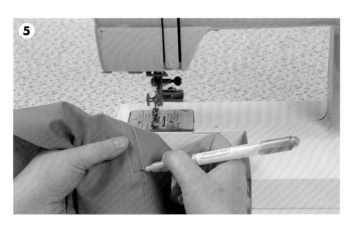

3. Pin the right side of the zipper on the seam, lining up the markings with where the zipper should start and stop. Make sure the zipper teeth run down the center of the seam.

4. Install the zipper foot on your machine and sew baste stitches on either side of the zipper teeth to hold the zipper in place.

5. On the right side of the fabric, use a water-soluble marking tool to mark the spot at the bottom of the zipper where you will pivot. This should be above the stop of the zipper itself and near where you did the backstitch.

6. Start at one side of the zipper and sew down to the mark you made in step 5. Pivot and sew across the zipper teeth at the bottom of the zipper. Pivot again, and sew to the top of the zipper. If the zipper pull gets in the way of stitching straight, remove some of the baste stitches to move the zipper.

7. Remove the baste stitches that were holding the zipper in place while sewing. Use your seam ripper to remove the baste stitches down the center of the seam.

8. Press the seam with an iron, being careful not to leave zipper teeth marks on the fabric.

HOW TO SEW AN INVISIBLE ZIPPER

Everyone who sews has a favorite closure, and for me it is the invisible zipper. I think it is the most professional way to insert a zipper, because there is no exterior stitching, so it looks just like a seam, as pictured on the back of this dress. The only part of the zipper you see in the end, if sewn correctly, is the top pull that is used to zip the zipper up and down. Prior to sewing the zipper into the garment, finish both sides of the seam allowance, as this is much harder to do after installing the zipper.

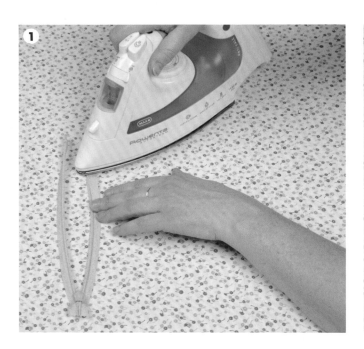

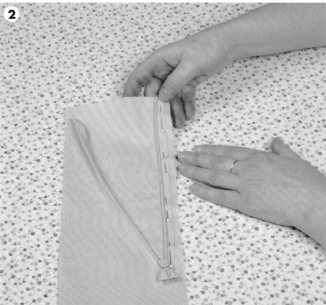

1. With the back side of the zipper up, press the teeth of the zipper so they are standing straight up. Do not over press them so they are flattened. They should be formed into a 90-degree angle with the zipper tape. As zippers are mostly plastic, be careful with the hot iron.

2. Place the left side of the zipper on the left side of the seam, right sides facing. This seam should be completely unsewn from top to bottom. Align the teeth of the zipper to the seam line specified in your pattern and pin in place.

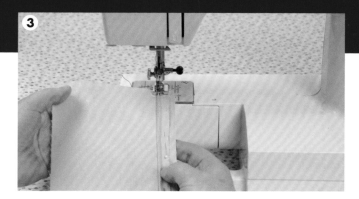

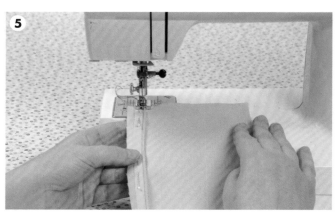

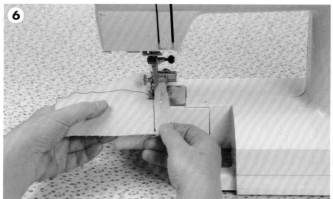

3. Switch from your regular presser foot to an invisible zipper foot. This is sometimes called a concealed zipper foot. Use the left channel of the zipper foot and line up the teeth into the groove. The right side of the seam should be in line with the seam allowance for the project. Sew a backstitch and sew all the way down until you are stopped by the zipper stop. Backstitch at the end as well.

4. Flip the zipper twice, placing it right-side down onto the right side of the other side of the seam. Pin in place, making sure the teeth are equal to the seam allowance distance from the side of the fabric.

5. Insert the zipper into the right channel of the invisible zipper foot. Use the left side seam allowance as your guide. If your machine does not have this, draw a line on the fabric to use as a guide for the zipper tape while sewing. Backstitch at the start and end of the stitch. Sew until you hit the stop at the bottom of the zipper.

6. Pin the end of the zipper tape out of the way of the seam allowance. Pin the remainder of the seam and install the regular zipper foot onto your machine. Beginning right where the stitching line ended when installing the zipper, sew a backstitch, and stitch the remainder of the seam.

7. Press the zipper seam open and finish the rest of the garment following the pattern instructions.

HOW TO SEW A LAPPED ZIPPER

A lapped zipper is often used in side seams and in the backs of skirts and dresses. It is like a centered zipper, except there is a flap of fabric that folds over the zipper teeth, making it a cleaner looking seam. This zipper incorporates the functionality of a regular zipper with the perks of an invisible zipper. Note that lapped zippers require a minimum of $5/8$" (1.5 cm) seam allowance.

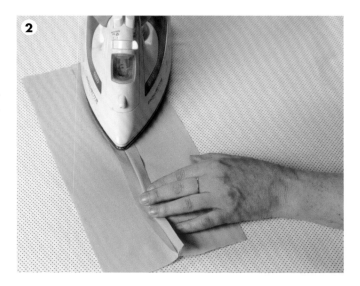

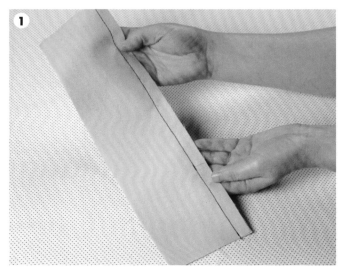

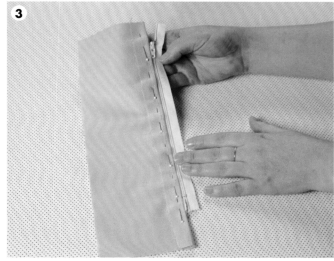

1. Consult the pattern and mark the bottom of the zipper placement accordingly. Sew with a baste stitch from the top of the seam until you reach the mark. Switch to a regular stitch, sew a backstitch, and continue with a regular stitch until you reach the bottom of the fabric.

2. Press the seam open with an iron set for your fabric type.

3. Fold the fabric so the seam is to the right and all the fabric and seam allowances are to the left. Gently roll the fabric to just expose a small amount of the right seam allowance. Place the zipper under the fabric and pin through all the layers.

4. Install a zipper foot on your machine and sew on the tiny part of fabric to the right of the seam. Opening up the zipper makes this step easier.

5. Turn the fabric right-side out. Pin the zipper and other seam allowance in place. Use a water-soluble marking tool to mark where the zipper end should be. Using a zipper foot, stitch from the top down to the bottom zipper mark, pivot, then sew across the zipper, ending with a backstitch.

6. Use a seam ripper to remove the baste stitches from step 1.

7. Give the zipper a press, taking care to use a pressing cloth to prevent marring the fabric with the teeth. Hiding under the flap of fabric is the zipper. Continue with the rest of the garment, following the instructions of your pattern.

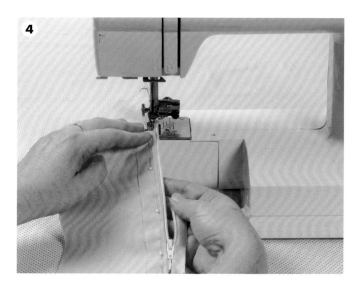

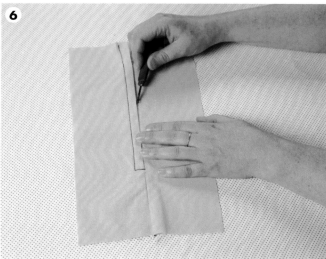

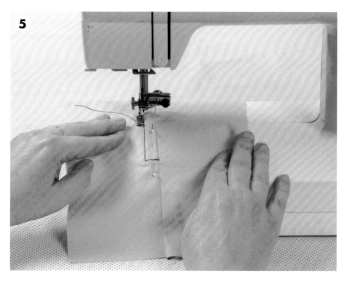

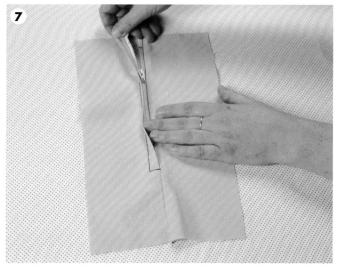

HOW TO SEW A FLY-FRONT ZIPPER

A fly-front zipper is one that is found on jeans, pants, some skirts, and shorts. It is the most challenging zipper insertion to master, as it is the least intuitive. But when done correctly, it is a lovely finish and one to be proud of. For this example, I am sewing a pair of fly-front pants; shorts will look the same. For a fly-front skirt, there will be some differences in the curve under the fly because it would go flat down the body and not under the crotch of the body.

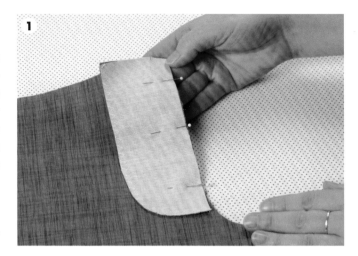

1. Follow the pattern instructions to interface and finish the edges of the fly facing. Pin the facing right sides together to the right pant front.

2. Sewing according to the seam allowance specified in the pattern, stitch the fly facing to the right pant front, stopping at the notch provided in the pattern.

3. Press the fly facing over and understitch just to the right of the seam sewn in step 2.

4. Prepare the fly extension by folding it in half, sewing the bottom, and finishing the unfolded edge. Switch to a zipper foot on your machine. Pin the zipper to the extension and sew, following the notch marks in the pattern instructions.

5. Pin the fly extension to the left pant front, lining up the zipper edge with the far left edge. The zipper should be trapped between the fly extension and the left pant front.

6. Using a zipper foot, sew through all the layers, stitching on top of your previous stitch. Stop at the notch provided by the pattern.

7. Turn the fly extension and press. Using a zipper foot, edge-stitch close to the seam, sewing through all the layers.

8. Following the markings and notches in the pattern, line up the right pant front and the left pant front, right sides together. Pin through the zipper and sew on the left side of the zipper, close to the teeth.

(continued)

4

4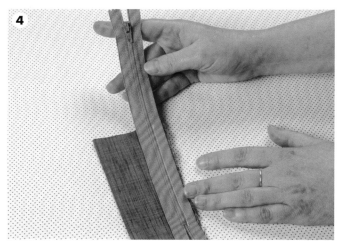

5

6

7

8

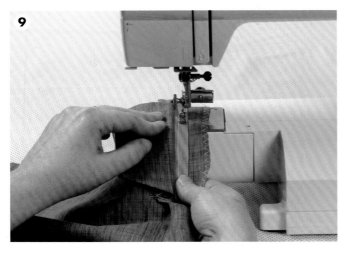

9. Stitch another row of stitches, this time on the right side of the zipper tape.

10. Fold the fly closed and flip to the right side of the pants. Using a seam gauge and water-soluble marking tool, draw the fly topstitching and curve. Pin all the layers together to keep in place. Stitch down the fly flap.

11. Continue sewing the fly flap, curving around the bottom of the fly.

12. Give the fly a press with the iron and continue to finish the project according to the pattern instructions.

How to Shorten a Zipper

Sometimes a project calls for a zipper length that you do not have on hand or one that is unavailable to you. If you have the proper type and color zipper, but the length is too long, you can simply shorten it by creating a new "stop" on the teeth by sewing zigzag stitches right over the teeth. Please note that if you are working with a zipper that has metal teeth, this is not to be done with a machine. Follow these same instructions, but do the sewing by hand instead of with the machine.

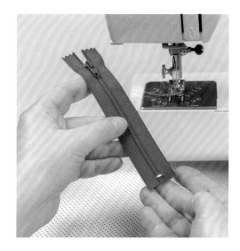

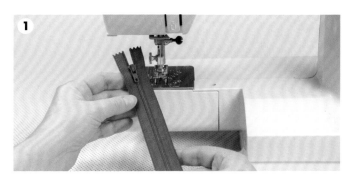

1. Get the zipper ready by making sure the tape is not wrinkled. Mark on the zipper where the new "stop" is to be sewn.

2. Insert the zipper into the machine. Set to a regular zigzag stitch with a width wide enough to cover one side of the zipper teeth to the other. Set the length to zero, as you do not want the stitch to move forward, only from side to side. Pass from side to side four or five times to make a secure spot on the zipper.

3. After it is sewn, it should have a thick bar tack of threads across the teeth of the zipper.

4. Trim the zipper below the new stop, leaving a little bit of length. If the zipper has metal teeth, do not use your sewing scissors to cut the zipper; use a metal cutting tool, such as wire cutters instead.

Finishing Seams

Most fabrics will fray and fall apart when laundered, disintegrating the seam allowance and possibly busting open the seams of your project. To keep this from happening, lock in the threads of the fabric by "finishing" them. There are many ways to do this with a standard home sewing machine, and the one you choose will likely be decided by where the seam is on the garment, what type of fabric you are using, and whether or not the seam allowance will be visible.

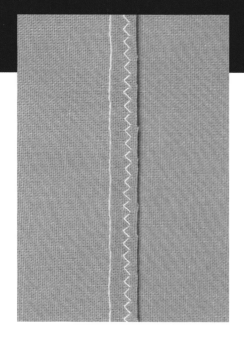

HOW TO SEW A ZIGZAG SEAM FINISH, METHOD 1

A very basic and easy, yet effective way to finish the seam allowance on medium-weight woven fabrics is with a simple zigzag stitch. This method involves sewing the zigzag stitch through both layers of the seam allowance, then trimming afterward.

1. After sewing a seam with a ⅝" (1.5 cm) seam allowance, insert the fabric back into the sewing machine on a ⅜" (1 cm) seam allowance. If the original seam allowance is different from ⅝" (1.5 cm), simply choose a seam allowance for the zigzag that is just to the outside of the straight stitch. Line up the right side with the seam allowance and insert the fabric so it is visible under the presser foot and aligned on top of the feed. Lower the presser foot.

2. There is no need for backstitching on a zigzag stitch, so simply sew straight along the chosen seam allowance until you reach the end of the seam.

3. Using a sharp pair of fabric scissors, trim off the excess seam allowance. Do not get too close to the zigzag stitch, as you could weaken it. Be sure to leave about ⅛" (3 mm) of fabric beside the zigzag finishing stitch.

4. Once the trimming is finished, press it with an iron adjusted to the setting for your fabric.

HOW TO SEW A ZIGZAG SEAM FINISH, METHOD 2

If you would prefer to have the seam allowance pressed open instead of pressed to one side and trimmed as in method 1, try this method, which is equally as effective as the first method. With a zigzag seam finish, you simply finish each side of the seam allowance individually.

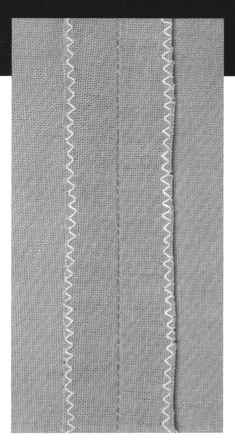

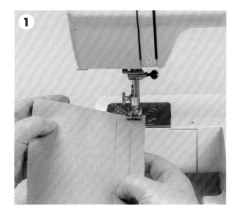

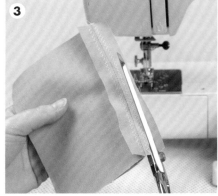

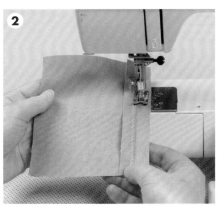

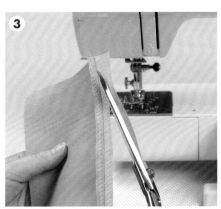

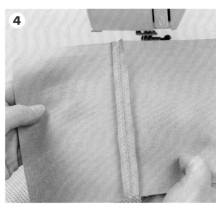

1. Insert one side of the seam allowance into the machine. Stitch the zigzag where you desire, either close to the seam as I am here, or near the edge of the seam allowance, as illustrated above.

2. Sew both sides of the seam allowance, locking the threads in place with the zigzag stitch. There is no need to backstitch the zigzag finishing stitch.

3. If you chose to stitch inside the seam allowance, trim off the excess fabric between the stitching and the edge of the seam allowance.

4. Give the seam a press, opening the seam and pressing the seam allowance to each side of the seam.

HOW TO SEW A 3-STEP ZIGZAG SEAM FINISH, METHOD 1

Much like a regular zigzag stitch, the 3-step zigzag stitch goes back and forth on the fabric. But because the 3-step is not just a single stitch from point to point, but rather three stitches from point to point, this finish tends to provide finer woven fabrics with a flatter finish than a regular zigzag gives. This finish is perfect for lightweight linen, cotton lawn, cotton voile, and similar weight fabrics. This version has the seam finishing stitches going through both layers of the seam allowance, then the excess is trimmed off afterward.

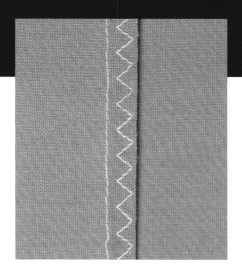

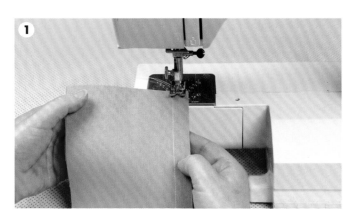

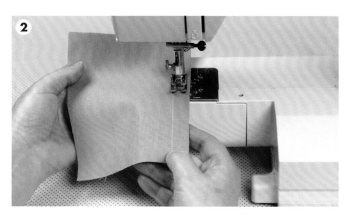

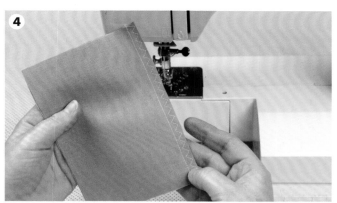

1. Place the fabric into the machine under the presser foot and on top of the feed. Line up the right side with a seam allowance that will have the 3-step zigzag falling just to the right of the straight stitch.

2. Do not backstitch at the beginning of the stitch; sew along the seam allowance until reaching the end of the seam.

3. After reaching the end of the seam, pull the fabric out, trim the threads, and use a sharp pair of fabric scissors to trim off the excess seam allowance. Leave behind about 1/8" (3 mm) of fabric between the 3-step zigzag and the trimmed edge.

4. Press the seam according to the project instructions, with the appropriate heat for the chosen fabric.

HOW TO SEW A 3-STEP ZIGZAG SEAM FINISH, METHOD 2

Much like with the regular zigzag finishing, the 3-step zigzag finish can be done through both layers of the fabric, as in method 1, or the sides of the seam allowance can be finished individually, so the seam can be pressed open. Depending on the fabric, project, and seam placement, one will be more appropriate than the other.

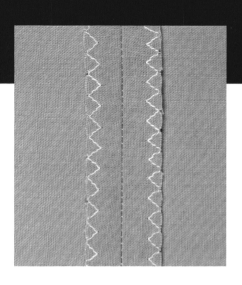

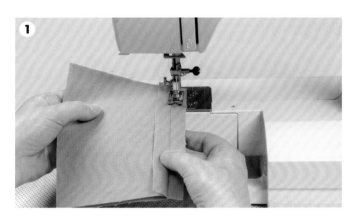

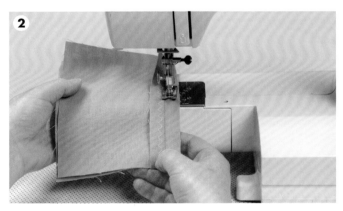

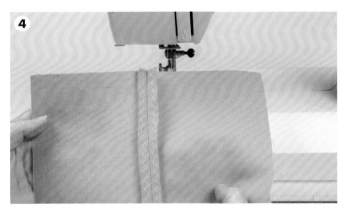

1. After sewing the seam, insert one side of the seam allowance into the machine. This can be stitched on the edge as pictured above, or in the middle with the excess trimmed off, as in this example.

2. Continue along the seam allowance until you have reached the end of the seam. Repeat on the other side of the seam.

3. If the zigzag stitch was placed anywhere on the seam allowance other than the outside edge, trim off the extra fabric close to the stitching.

4. Press the seam open, keeping the seam allowances on each side of the seam.

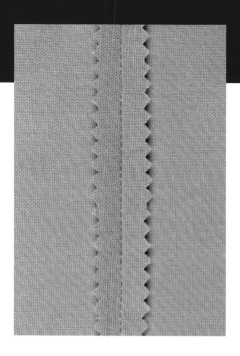

HOW TO FINISH A SEAM WITH PINKING SCISSORS

If you have ever seen a handmade vintage garment, you might have noticed that all of the seams on the inside were cut with a zigzag finish. This is done with pinking scissors. The blades on pinking scissors have pointy teeth that create a series of mountain peaks and valleys along the fabric. Believe it or not, when many woven fabrics are cut with these scissors, the fabric will not fray, making this a quick and easy way to finish the seams of a project.

Note that not all fabrics like to be cut with these scissors, so it is best to test them on a scrap prior to using them on your project. Most synthetic fabrics do not cut in a crisp manner with pinking scissors, but cottons, linens, and other woven natural fibers usually take to them very well.

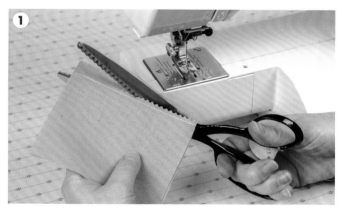

1. Once you have sewn your seam, simply cut along the side of the straight seam with your pinking scissors. Visualize that you want to leave behind about ⅛" (3 mm) of fabric beside the straight stitch. If necessary, use a chalk pencil and ruler to draw a line to cut along.

2. As with all other seam finishing, press the finished seam according to the project instructions and use the appropriate iron setting for your fabric.

BOUND HONG KONG SEAM FINISHING

A Hong Kong seam finish is ideal for thick or heavy fabrics that have a loose weave structure and need extra support to prevent raveling. Cut bias strips to make the binding, or use store-bought bias tape. If using the premade variety, be sure to press out all manufacturer folds before using.

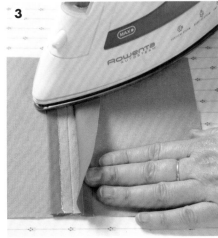

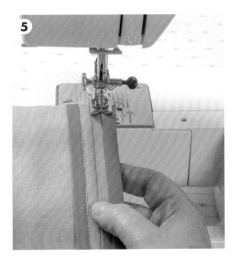

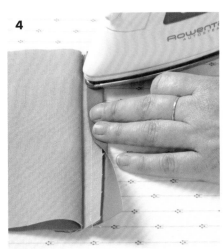

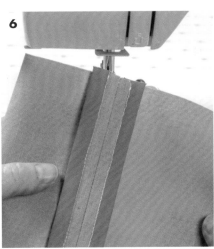

1. The seam should already be sewn and the wrong side of the fabric is up. Pin the binding to one side of the seam allowance's outer edge.

2. Sew the binding to the outer edge at a ¼" (6 mm) seam allowance. For this step, I used a ¼" (6 mm) seam foot on my machine.

3. Press the binding seam open toward the side of the seam allowance on which you are stitching.

4. Fold and press the remaining width of the binding to the underside of the seam allowance, encasing the entire edge of the seam allowance in the binding.

5. Stitch on the top side of the seam allowance, close to the seam where the binding connects to the seam allowance.

6. Press the binding and the seam allowance with an iron set to the heat for your project. Use a pressing cloth if necessary.

SELF-BOUND SEAM FINISHING

A self-bound seam finish is an elegant approach for getting a minimal seam allowance on the inside of your garment. This method is perfect for lightweight fabrics and for those that do not ravel quickly; a fabric that frays easily will not hold a self-bound seam well.

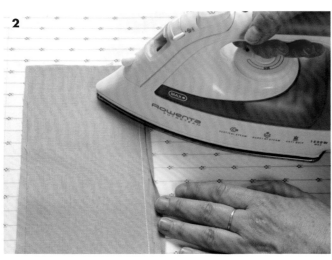

1. The seam is already sewn and the wrong side of the project is facing up. Fold the seam in half so all the fabric is to one side and both seam allowances are off to the other side. Trim the seam allowance on top down to $1/8$" (3 mm), being careful not to cut the other seam allowance.

2. Fold and press the wider seam allowance $1/8$" (3 mm) in the direction of the seam.

3. Fold the wider seam allowance a second time, another $1/8$" (3 mm), lining it up with the first row of stitches.

4. Stitch along the last fold, keeping all the excess fabric off to the left and only the seam allowance in the machine.

5. Press the entire seam flat with an iron set for the fabric you are using.

HOW TO SEW A FRENCH SEAM

French seams are a beautiful way to finish the inside of any garment. This method is especially perfect for thin or sheer fabrics where seeing the seam allowance would ruin the appearance. Sewing French seams for the first time always feels backward, because you start with wrong sides together, instead of the usual right sides together, but in the end it is a lovely and addictive approach to finishing your handmade garments in an elegant and professional manner.

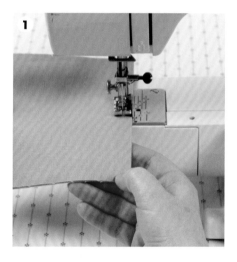

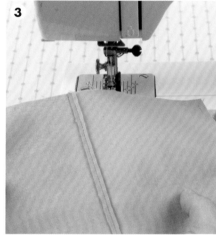

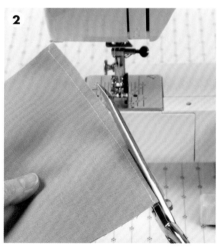

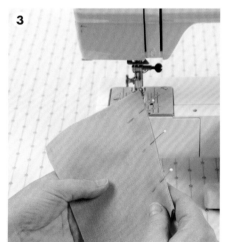

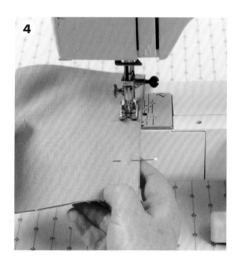

1. Sew with wrong sides together, and right sides out, on the ⅜" (1 cm) seam allowance.

2. Trim the seam allowances down to ⅛" (3 mm).

3. Open up the seam and fold the right sides together. Pin in place.

4. Reinsert the fabric into the machine, this time with right sides facing, and sew the additional amount to total the project's seam allowance.

5. Press on the wrong side of the fabric, pressing the French seam to one side depending on the pattern's instructions.

HOW TO SEW A FLAT-FELL SEAM

A flat-fell seam is most commonly found on button-down dress shirts for men and on jeans. It has an exposed stitch on the right side, and a clean, folded, and stitched-down seam allowance on the inside. This method is quite simple to do on straight seams, but can be tricky on curves and armholes.

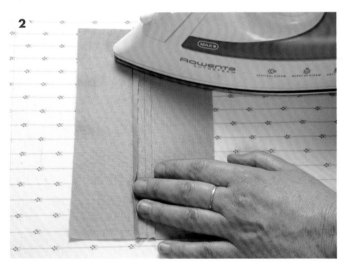

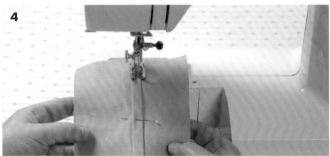

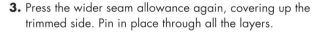

1. Sew the seam with the wrong sides together and the seam allowance pressed open on the right side of the fabric. Trim one side of the seam allowance down to ¼" (6 mm) but do not trim the other side.

2. Fold the wider seam allowance toward the seam and press.

3. Press the wider seam allowance again, covering up the trimmed side. Pin in place through all the layers.

4. Stitch on the right side through all layers, close to the fold.

5. Press the seam flat with an iron set to an appropriate heat for your fabric.

Sewing Curves

If you picture a circle or curve, the outer edge is wider, or longer, than the inner edge, much like a racetrack. So when curves are folded in one direction or the other, the curve needs to be either clipped to spread out, or notched to fit in. A curve will not lie flat if the seam allowance is not treated in one of these ways. It is a good idea to sew a staystitch before clipping or notching into the fabric to keep the threads secure and strong. Clipping and notching will be necessary on all curves, including necklines, armholes, and princess seams.

CLIPPING CURVES

If the smaller edge of a curve is folded in the direction of a wider curve, it needs to be clipped. Clipping consists of cutting small lines into the curve, allowing the clipped spots to open and spread so that the seam can lie flat. Always clip less than you think you should, then progress more and more until the seam lies flat. The seam will weaken if it is clipped too much or if it is clipped too close to the seam allowance.

CUTTING NOTCHES

In the opposite direction, if the wider edge of a curve is folded into a smaller area, the fabric will buckle and fold in on itself. Notches are triangle wedges of fabric that are cut from the curve to allow the fabric to fit inside the smaller curve that it has been folded into. As with clipping, always notch less than you think you should, then cut additional amounts as needed to keep the seam as strong as possible.

Sewing Pivots

There are many instances when you need to pivot on your fabric while sewing a project. These include making collars, sewing scalloped hems, and many other similiar situations. The key is to always keep the needle in the fabric when lifting the presser foot, enabling you to stay in position on your fabric at all times.

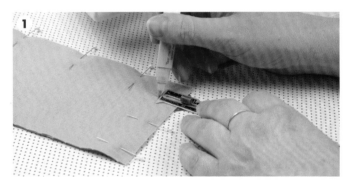

1. Use a water-soluble marking tool to mark the pivot spot at the seam allowance for the item you are sewing.

2. If the stitch is going down the right side, as in my example, my pivot mark is parallel to the other side, informing me when I am the proper seam allowance distance from the other side.

3. Sew along the first side and approach the pivot spot.

4. Stop sewing just short of the mark and manually turn the hand wheel toward you to stitch until the needle is on the pivot line.

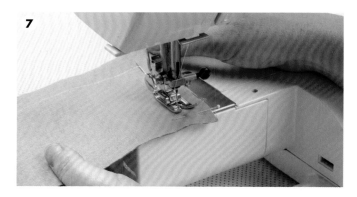

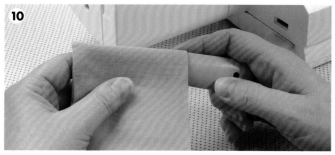

5. Sink the needle into the pivot line and lift the presser foot.

6. Pivot the fabric and line up the other side of the fabric with the seam allowance. If you are not yet at the seam allowance, pivot the fabric back where you started, lower the presser foot, and manually move forward another stitch. If you fear that one full stitch will put you beyond the pivot mark, simply turn down the stitch length to a shorter amount and turn the hand wheel until the needle is on the proper seam allowance.

7. Continue sewing the rest of the stitch.

8. A properly sewn pivot should form a nice, crisp corner and be equidistant from the seam allowance on each side of the stitching.

9. To reduce bulk on the corner, clip off the right angle before turning the fabric right-side out. Additional trimming might be necessary on either side of the corner if the fabric used is too bulky.

10. Turn the fabric right-side out. Use a point turner to gently push out the seam allowance in the corner.

Grading and Trimming Seams

Seam allowances are built into a project for the ease of sewing. But once the project is sewn, the seam allowance is only there to keep the stitch secure. Any excess fabric that is inside the project can be trimmed if it is creating bulk around the body.

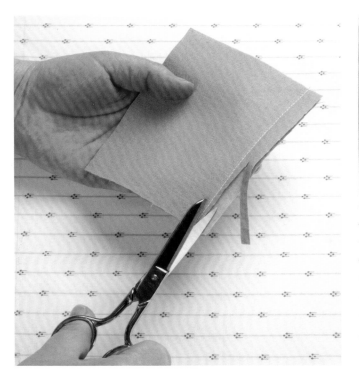 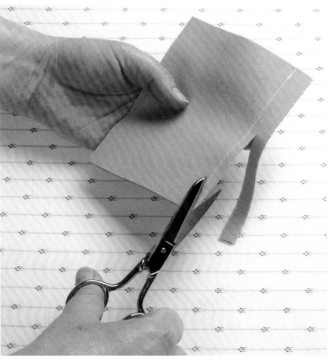

HOW TO GRADE A SEAM

Grading is the art of trimming the seam allowances inside the garment at different lengths to create a smooth and bulk-free look on the right side. To grade a seam, simply trim the seam allowances at a series of tiered widths. In my example, there are only two fabrics intersecting, but if it were a neckline with a flat collar, there might be four or more fabrics in the seam. Each one can be trimmed at a slightly less amount, starting at a full ⅝" (1.5 cm) seam allowance, and ending at a slim ⅛" (3 mm) width. The longest seam allowance should be whichever edge is facing out, so the seam appears smooth.

HOW TO TRIM A SEAM

Trimming a seam is as simple as cutting the seam allowance to whatever width you would like. This is usually done in conjunction with seam finishing, so the integrity of the fabric stays intact and is not weakened by raveling.

Sewing with Knits

Knit fabrics are unlike woven fabrics in that the threads are knitted together to create a fabric with stretch. Because the fabric stretches, it cannot be sewn the same way as a fabric without stretch. If a straight stitch is sewn on nonstretch fabrics, both the stitch and the fabric remain inactive. But if a straight stitch is sewn on knit fabric, the thread will snap when the garment is stretched.

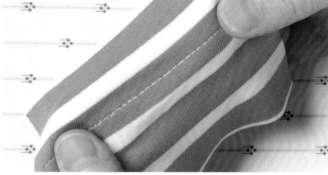

This is an example of what happens when a straight stitch on a knit fabric is pulled. The thread will snap and break, busting open the seam.

If you use a stretch straight stitch setting on knit fabric, it will stay intact when pulled and stretch along with the fabric.

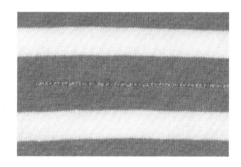

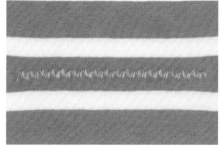

If your machine offers stretch stitches, one of them will be a straight-stretch stitch. With this stitch the machine sews two stitches forward and one stitch back, then repeats this motion, allowing the stitch to stretch with the knit fabric. This is also a handy stitch for reinforcing areas on woven fabrics that are typically strained during wear, like crotch or underarm seams.

A stretch zigzag stitch is much like a stretch-straight stitch, in that it reinforces the stitch by moving a stitch forward and then back, to allow for stretch within the stitch.

For hemming, the honeycomb stitch is a nice option that lies really flat on the fabric, making a clean hem on knit fabrics. It is also good for securing elastic to knits for waistbands.

Anatomy of a Garment

Sewing with knits (1)	Topstitching (6)
Flat collar (2)	Straight stretch stitch (7)
Clipping curves (3)	Elastic waist casing (8)
Seam grading (4)	Honeycomb stretch stitch (9)
Understitching (5)	Knit sewn hem (10)

Sewing curves (1)	Set-in sleeve (6)
Neckline facings (2)	Bust and waist darts (7)
Seam grading (3)	Double fold sleeve hem (8)
Understitching (4)	Knife pleats (9)
Invisible zipper (5)	Hand stitched hem (10)

Flat collar (1)	Flat buttons (6)
Neckline facings (2)	Gathered sleeve (7)
Understitching (3)	Double fold sleeve hem (8)
Topstitching (4)	Bust darts (9)
Buttonholes (5)	Double fold shirt hem (10)

Sewing with knits (1)	Elastic waist casing
Clipping curves (2)	(leggings) (5)
Bias neckline binding (3)	Double fold dress hem (6)
Bias binding sleeveless	Matching stripes (7)
finishing (4)	

TAKING SHAPE

Once the fabric and pattern have been selected and cut out, and decisions have been made as to how you want to assemble the garment, it is time to begin forming the fabric into the elements that will shape the item's style and details. In this chapter we will get familiar with the common elements found in garment construction, including darts, pleats, gathers, collars, and sleeves. These are the elements that will form your finished garment to the body and add interest and style.

Darts

A dart is a fold in the fabric that allows curves in the body to fill the three-dimensional shape that the fold creates. The dart is shaped much like a triangle. The point is called the "apex" and the lines coming from the point are the "legs." Poorly sewn and pressed darts will result in puckering at the apex, which make for particularly unflattering bumps on the body, especially in bust darts. The goal is to create smooth, undulating waves that glide over the body's curves.

BASIC DART

1. With the pattern piece pinned to the fabric, and the wrong side of the fabric facing you, peel back the right corner of the right dart leg. Using a water-soluble pencil, mark the intersection of the line and the edge of the fabric with a small dash or dot. Be sure to use the appropriate line for the size you are sewing.

2. Repeat step 1 on the left dart leg.

3. Place a pin into the apex of the dart, inserting the pin through the pattern and the fabric, into the point of the size you are making.

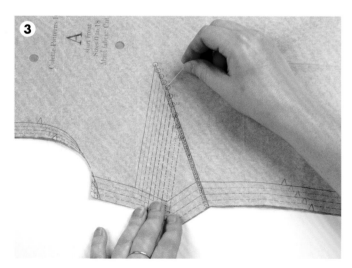

4

6

5

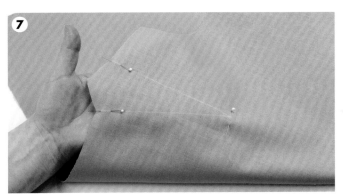

7

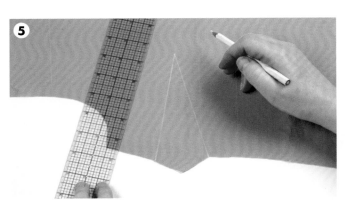

5

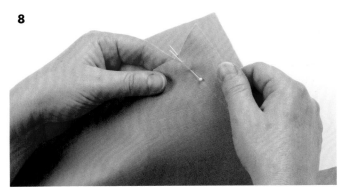

8

4. Gently lift the pattern over the pin that is placed into the apex of the dart. Use the water-soluble pencil to make a small dot at the base of the pin, where it is inserted into the fabric.

5. Using a clear ruler and water-soluble pencil, connect the dart legs with the dart apex.

6. Insert a pin through the fabric at the apex of the dart. This should be through just the single layer upon which the dart is drawn.

7. Insert a pin into each of the dart legs. Place the pin heads toward the apex and allow the pin points to hang over the fabric edge.

8. Fold the right sides of the fabric together, and with the apex in your right hand, bring the pin point ends and the dart legs together. Lift out the pin facing you and while staying in line with the dart legs, pin through both layers of the fabric. Flip the fabric over to make sure the pin is through the line on the back of the dart. If not, remove the pin and shift the fabric until the pin is perfectly through both dart legs. Remove the pin from the back of the dart.

(continued)

9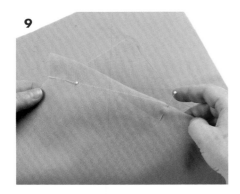

10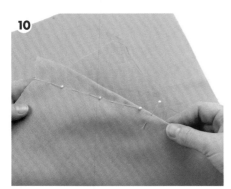

10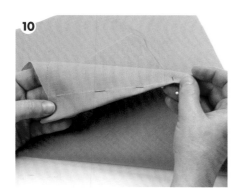

11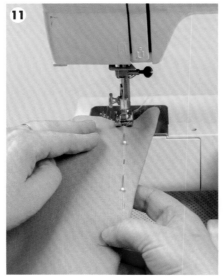

12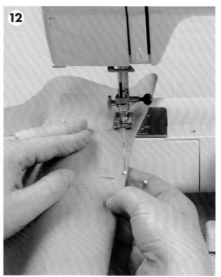

13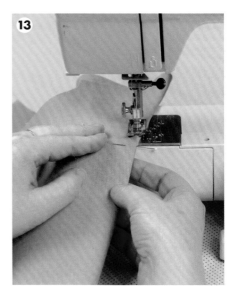

14

9. With the fabric folded, remove the din at the apex and pin through both layers to make a fold.

10. Place pins through the rest of the dart, making sure they are in line with the dart legs on both sides of the fabric.

11. Place the dart into the sewing machine with the apex facing you and excess fabric to the left of the machine. Before sewing, make sure all pin heads are facing you so they are easy to remove while sewing. Sew a backstitch at the beginning of the dart.

12. Continue sewing along the dart legs, keeping in line with the chalk marks. Remove the pins as you approach them.

13. Stop sewing about ½" (1.3 cm) before the apex of the dart. Reduce your stitch length to 1.0. Continue sewing along the dart, finally going off the fabric at the end. Do not backstitch.

14. Clip the threads close to the apex. Do not tie the threads together, as this will create an unwanted bump.

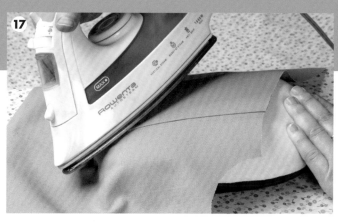

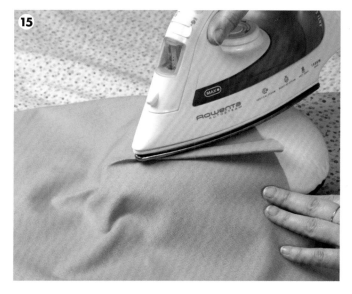

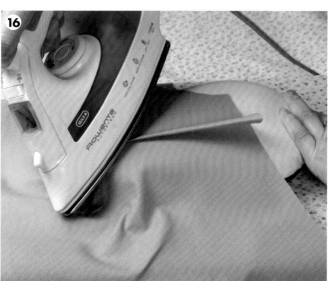

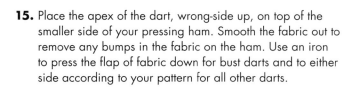

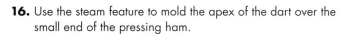

15. Place the apex of the dart, wrong-side up, on top of the smaller side of your pressing ham. Smooth the fabric out to remove any bumps in the fabric on the ham. Use an iron to press the flap of fabric down for bust darts and to either side according to your pattern for all other darts.

16. Use the steam feature to mold the apex of the dart over the small end of the pressing ham.

17. Repeat the pressing steps on the right side of your fabric. Use a press cloth if working with a delicate fabric.

18. A perfectly sewn dart will look like a clean, smooth seam with a pucker-free apex. If necessary, redampen the dart apex and repress until smooth.

CONTOUR DARTS

A contour dart looks like two darts back to back, and that is exactly what it is. The widest part of the first dart faces the widest part of the second dart, so the legs of the dart meet in the middle, forming a diamond shape. There are two apexes, one on each end of the diamond. Contour darts are commonly found near the waist to give the garment some shaping around the middle of the body. Making these darts is essentially like sewing two separate darts.

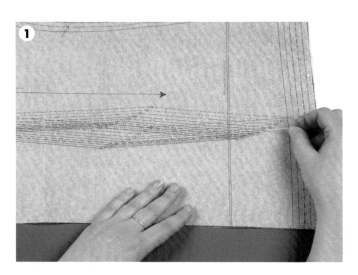

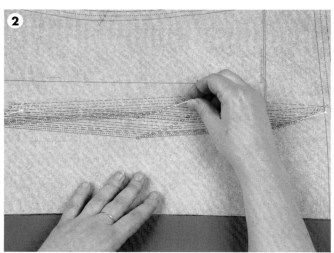

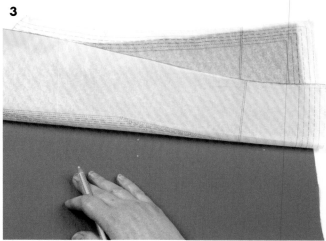

1. With the pattern pinned in place and the wrong side of the fabric facing you, place a pin through the right apex. Use the appropriate dot for the size garment you are making. Repeat on the left apex.

2. Insert pins through the other two size markings, where the two dart legs connect.

3. Carefully lift the pattern up along the pins. Using a water-soluble pencil, mark the intersection of the pin and the fabric with a dot.

4

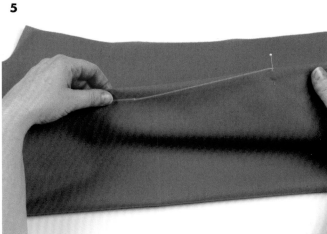

4

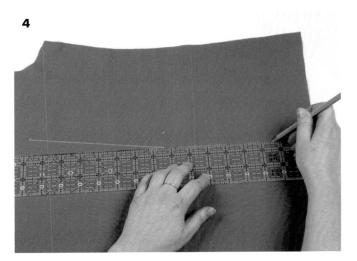

5

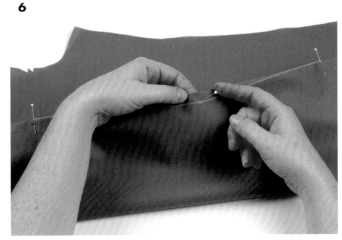

6

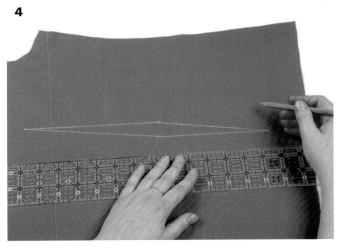

4. On the wrong side of the fabric, use a clear ruler and a water-soluble pencil to connect the dart apex and dart legs to form a diamond shape.

5. Exactly as you would with a regular dart, fold the fabric and place a pin through all the layers at the right apex, perpendicular with the dart. Repeat on the left side.

6. Insert a pin through the ends of the dart legs, where they intersect at the center of the dart. Shift the fabric until the pin is lined up on both sides of the fabric.

(continued)

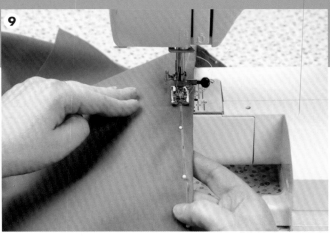

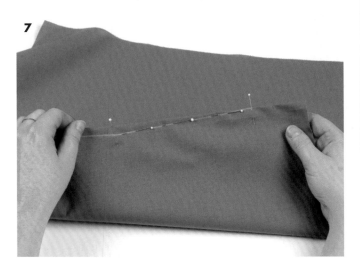

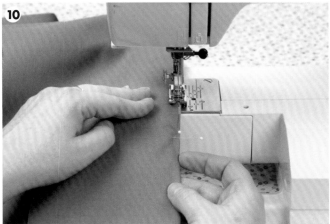

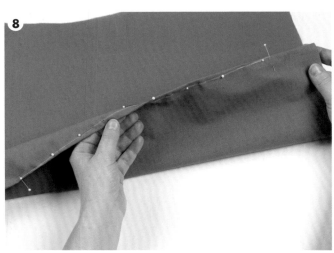

7. Insert the pins through both sides of the right dart, lining them up with the chalk lines. Arrange the pin heads to face the apex.

8. Repeat the previous step on the left dart, on the opposite side of the fabric so the pins are facing the apex and the excess fabric is off to the left of the dart.

9. Take the fabric to the sewing machine. Starting at the center of the dart, backstitch and sew toward the apex, along the chalk line.

10. Stop about ½" (1.3 cm) before the apex of the dart. Turn your stitch length down to 1.0 for the remainder of the dart. Continue along the line, sewing off the fabric at the apex. Do not backstitch.

11. Clip the threads close to the apex. Do not tie the threads together as it will leave a bump in the fabric when pressed. Repeat this process on the other side of the dart, backstitching at the center and sewing off at the apex with a 1.0 stitch length.

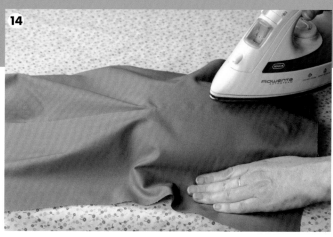

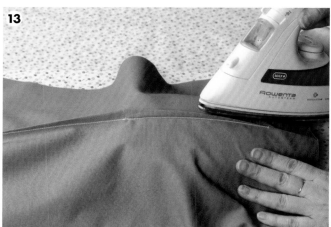

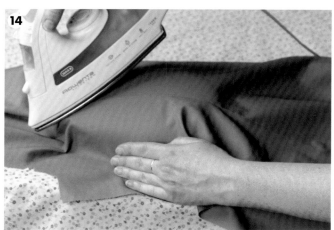

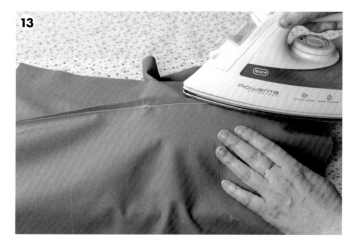

12. Clip the seam allowance at the center of the dart, stopping just short of the stitching.

13. As with a regular dart, place your pressing ham under the dart and press according to the project instructions. Place the smaller side of the ham at the apex of the dart and smooth out until free of puckers and bumps. Repeat on the other side of the dart.

14. Flip the garment over and press on the right side of the fabric. Use a pressing cloth for delicate fabrics.

15. Press using the ham until the contour dart is a smooth seam and the apex points are free of unwanted puckers.

FRENCH DARTS

A French dart looks much like a regular dart, except the triangle that forms the dart is significantly longer and originates at a side seam around the waist or hip on the body. It usually has a slight curve, forming a long skinny curved triangle with the apex at the bust, just like a regular dart. The biggest difference in sewing a French dart versus a regular dart is that the fabric is trimmed down after it is sewn, reducing the bulk along the dart and at the side seam. A well-sewn French dart will result in a smooth apex and a side seam that lines up perfectly once it is sewn and pressed.

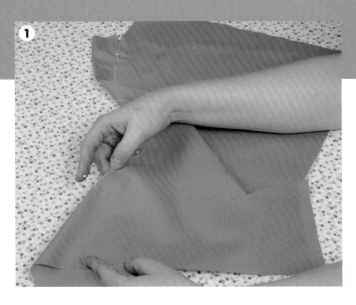

1. Draw the lines of the dart onto your fabric in the same method as a regular bust dart. Once the dart is drawn, fold the fabric at the dart apex, right sides together, and insert a pin through all layers.

2. Pin along the chalk line, placing the pins through the lines of the dart legs, and make sure the pins align on both sides of the fabric.

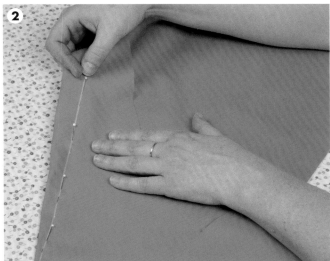

3. At the end of the dart, the stitching line will line up with the fabric and the dart fabric will hang off the edge.

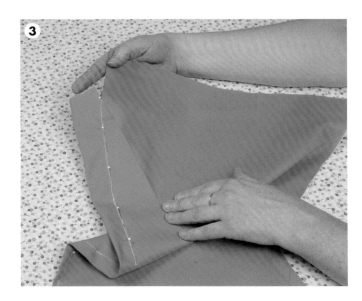

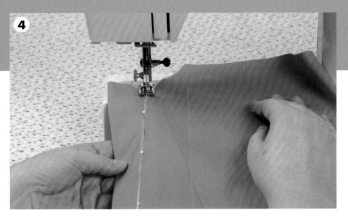

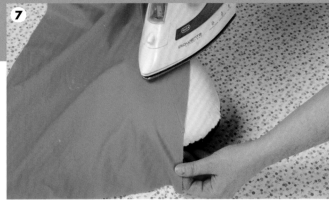

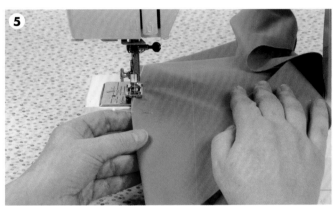

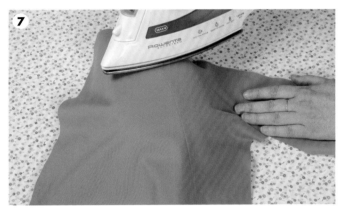

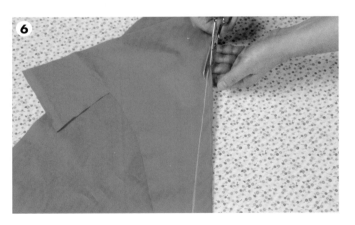

4. Starting at the end of the dart, backstitch and sew along the chalk line. Remove pins along the line as you approach them.

5. About ½" (1.3 cm) before the apex of the dart, stop and turn your stitch length down to 1.0. Continue along the line of your dart off the fabric. Do not backstitch. Clip the thread ends close to the fabric. Due to the tight stitch length, the stitch will hold and last without knotting the thread or backstitching.

6. Trim the dart seam allowance down from the apex to the bottom.

7. Place a pressing ham under the dart and press the dart with the seam allowance in the direction required for the project you are sewing.

8. Just as with a regular dart, a French dart should be a smooth seam, ending in a pucker-free apex.

Gathering

Gathering is the art of taking a piece fabric that is too wide for what it will be sewn to and reducing it to fit. This is a technique that can be found nearly everywhere, from skirts, to tops, to pillows, and bed skirts. Look around and you will see gathering all over the place, so it is a very handy technique to master. To create gathers, you sew two rows of basting stitches on the larger fabric, pull the fabric along those threads—much like you would move curtains along a curtain rod—then pin and sew them in place.

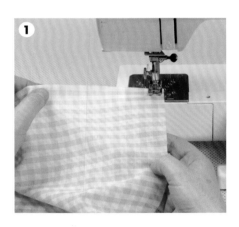

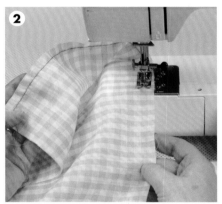

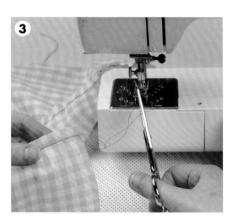

1. Set your stitch length to 4.0 or 5.0 for baste stitching and insert the fabric into the machine ⅛" (3 mm) above the seam allowance. In this example, the stitch is on ½" (1.3 cm) as the seam allowance is ⅝" (1.5 cm).

2. Start the baste stitch with long threads and stitch all the way to the other side. Do not backstitch on either end as you want the stitch to move and backstitching would hold it in place.

3. At the end of the baste stitch, leave long threads to use for gathering.

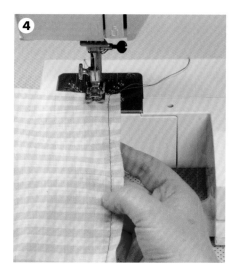

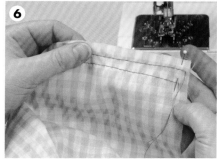

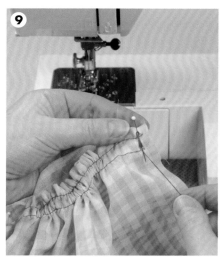

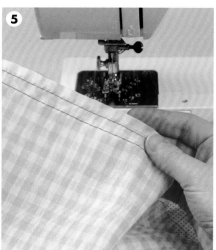

4. Line up the second row of baste stitches ⅛" (3 mm) farther from the edge than the project's seam allowance. For the example shown, the seam allowance is ⅝" (1.5 cm) and the baste stitches are sewn ¾" (1.9 cm) from the edge.

5. As with the first line of baste stitches, leave long threads at the start and do not backstitch. Use the same long stitch length and sew to the other end of the fabric. Leave long threads again and do not backstitch.

6. Line up the left and right sides of the gathered item with the piece to which it is being gathered. Make sure right sides are facing.

7. Find the center of the gathered item and match it up with the center of the piece to which it is being gathered. Pin together at the centers.

8. Separate the threads facing you from the threads on the other side of the baste stitches. Hold onto the two threads facing you and slide the fabric down the threads, gathering them up between the pinned end and the center point.

9. Once the gathering has reduced the two pieces to the same size from side pin to center pin, use the threads you were holding to create a figure eight around the pin on the end. This will hold the threads in place and keep them from shifting.

(continued)

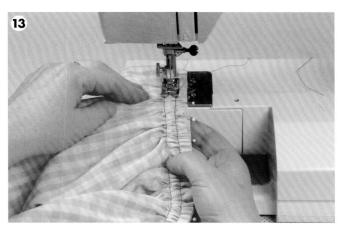

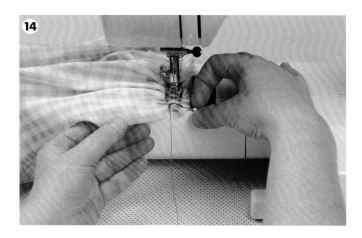

10. Repeat steps 8 and 9 for the other half of the gathered piece. Even out the gathering by sliding the fabric along the baste stitches. Try to make them as consistent as possible, otherwise there will be bunches or blank spots along the seam after it is sewn.

11. Once the gathering is even, pin the two pieces together, aligning the top edges. Repeat on the rest of the item to be gathered until the whole item is gathered and pinned in place.

12. Insert the gathering into the sewing machine with the gathering facing up. Sink the needle of the machine into the fabric. Once held in place, take out the pin on the end that has the threads secured to it. Separate the baste threads so you do not sew over them when stitching the items together.

13. Sew along your seam allowance, which, if done correctly, should have you sewing between the two rows of baste stitches. Keep the gathers in place as you go over them and remove the pins just as you approach them.

14. Sew to the other end and stop just before the pin on the end with the threads secured. Sink your needle into the fabric.

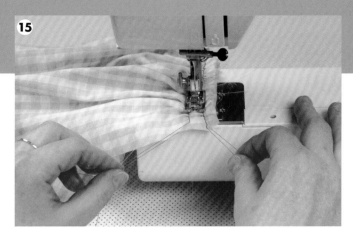

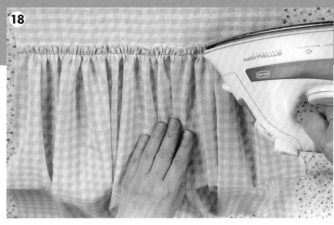

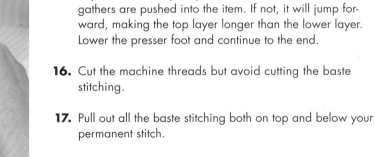

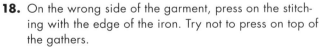

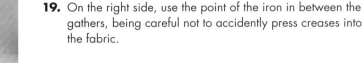

15. Separate the threads as you did at the beginning, to move them out of the way for sewing. With your needle in your fabric, lift your presser foot and make sure all gathers are pushed into the item. If not, it will jump forward, making the top layer longer than the lower layer. Lower the presser foot and continue to the end.

16. Cut the machine threads but avoid cutting the baste stitching.

17. Pull out all the baste stitching both on top and below your permanent stitch.

18. On the wrong side of the garment, press on the stitching with the edge of the iron. Try not to press on top of the gathers.

19. On the right side, use the point of the iron in between the gathers, being careful not to accidently press creases into the fabric.

ELASTIC GATHERING IN CASING

A casing is a fold in the fabric that is sewn down to make a channel. This channel can be filled with a drawstring or elastic to cinch up the fabric. Peek at a pair of pajama bottoms and there will likely be a waist casing with something inside. To fill the casing with elastic, an opening is left near the start of the seam and elastic is inserted. This can be used for skirt or pant waists, pant hems, or necklines. A skirt waist is shown in this example.

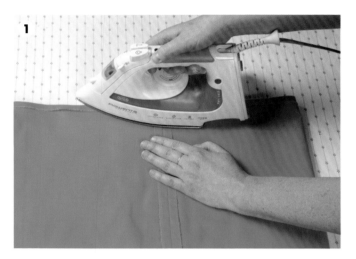

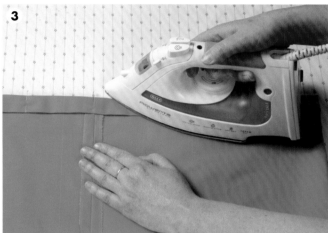

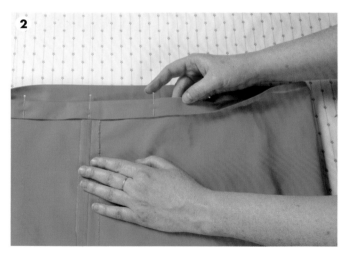

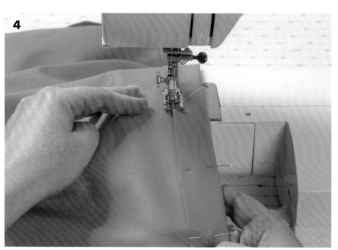

1. Once your side seams are sewn, turn the garment wrong-side out. Fold the top raw edge of the item down ¼" (6 mm) and press.

2. Fold the top down a second time and pin in place. Avoid using plastic head pins, as these will melt under the heat of the iron when pressed. Use a seam gauge to fold enough to fit the elastic inside. The casing should be about ¼" (6 mm) larger than the elastic width.

3. Press the pinned edge with an iron.

4. Using a straight stitch, sew close to the inner fold. Start at a side seam and stop 2" (5.1 cm) before you reach your starting point. Backstitch at both the start and the finish, as the opening will be pulled on when inserting the elastic.

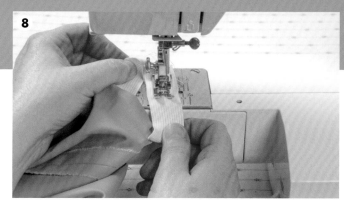

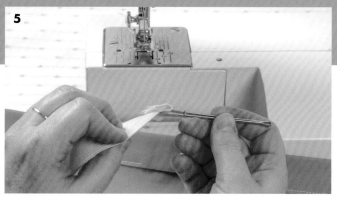

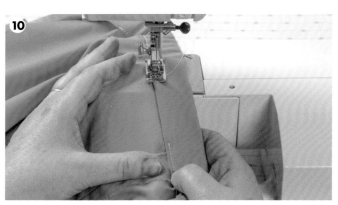

5. Fold the end of your elastic and attach it to a bodkin. Tighten the stopper on the bodkin to hold the elastic tight.

6. Insert the bodkin into the opening and feed it through the casing. In order to gather up the waist, the elastic will be shorter in diameter than the waist, so be careful not to lose the end of the elastic in the casing while feeding the bodkin through. As the elastic end draws close, secure it in place with a pin.

7. Once you have gone all the way around the waist, pull the two ends of the elastic out of the opening and remove the bodkin. Overlap the ends of the elastic 1" (2.5 cm) and pin together. Make sure the elastic did not twist during the insertion process.

8. Place the elastic under the presser foot and lower the needle into it to secure. Use a zigzag stitch to stitch forward and back along the width of the overlapping twice.

9. Fit the elastic into the casing through the opening on the waist.

10. Align with the previous stitching on the opening and close up the hole left in the waist.

ELASTIC GATHERING WITHOUT A CASING

Sometimes a design will call for an elastic finish, but without a casing to hold the elastic. Rather than enclosed inside, the neighboring edge is finished, and then the elastic is applied just inside the edge. This is commonly found on paper-bag style waists and long sleeve hems. Because there is no casing to hold the elastic, it must be stretched as it is sewn to the woven fabric.

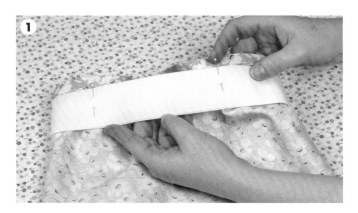

1. Finish the seam according to the pattern instructions. On this example, I have finished the sleeve with a double fold and topstitched hem. Cut the elastic to the desired length. Overlap the ends of the elastic by 1" (2.5 cm) and sew together using a zigzag stitch. Divide the fabric into four equal parts and mark each spot with chalk. Repeat on the elastic. Line up the elastic on the fabric and pin in place at each of those four spots, evenly distributing the elastic around the fabric. If the item is especially wide, more than four spots of pinning is recommended.

2. Place the elastic and fabric into the sewing machine. If the elastic used is ½" (1.3 cm) wide or smaller, use a single straight stitch through the center of the elastic. If the elastic used is wider than ½" (1.3 cm) the elastic will be more

secure if two rows of stitching are used, one at the top and one at the bottom. Sink the needle into the elastic and sew a backstitch to secure. Sink the needle back into the fabric and pull the elastic at the back and the front until it matches the width of the fabric. Sew from the first pin to the second. Repeat by stretching and sewing around the entire item until you have reached the starting point. Secure with another backstitch.

3. If the elastic is wider than ½" (1.3 cm) repeat the sewing on the other end of the elastic. Use the same stretch and sew method as was used in step 2.

4. The finished result will be evenly distributed gathers on the right side of the garment, with an elastic finish on the inside.

Pleating

Pleats are nothing more than folds in the fabric that are sewn into place, but those simple folds can be formed in many ways and can create tremendous impact. Pleats and gathers are similar in that a wider piece of fabric is being reduced to fit a smaller piece of fabric. While gathers create a soft edge, pleats have a crisp and slightly more formal feeling. Most edges that call for gathers can be substituted for pleats and vice versa, so give them a try on your next project.

KNIFE PLEATS

Knife pleats have a single fold line and consecutive pleats are folded in the same direction. Some patterns might have sets of knife pleats facing in or out of a central point. Follow the pattern's instructions as to which direction the pleats should go.

1. Following the markings on the pattern, mark the pleat folds with water-soluble chalk.

1

2

2. Insert pins into the chalk marks, leaving the heads of the pins extended above the edge of the fabric so they are easy to see. Do not use pins with plastic heads, as they will melt under the heat of the iron.

3

3. Fold the fabric, lining up the first pin with the second pin to form the knife pleat.

4

4. Pin through all the layers with two pins, one on either side of the pleat, to secure it in place.

(continued)

5

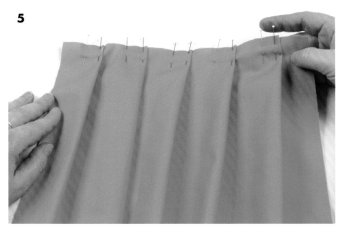

6

7

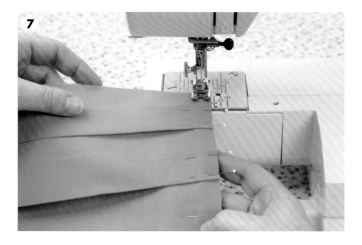

8

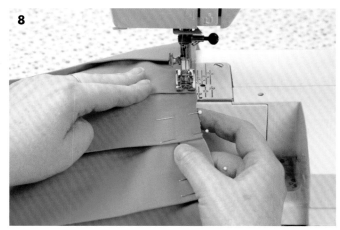

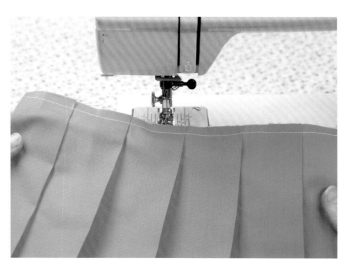

5. Repeat with the rest of the folds and pin in place.

6. Use an iron to press on the pleat, from the top of the fabric to just below the project's seam allowance, so the area about to be sewn is smooth and flat.

7. Stitch along the pleats with a baste stitch, just short of the project's seam allowance. For this example, the project calls for a ⅝" (1.5 cm) seam allowance and I am stitching it at the ⅜" (1 cm) mark.

8. Continue sewing around the entire pleated piece, being careful to keep the folds on both the top and the bottom layer of the fabric flat. Give the piece a final press on top of the stitching before sewing the pleats into a seam.

INVERTED PLEATS

Inverted pleats have two fold lines that meet up at a central spot. The fabric between the two fold lines is evenly distributed behind the fold lines, creating two additional fold lines that face opposite each other. This type of pleat creates a flat looking front, only to reveal a pleated underside when opened or when moved while wearing.

3

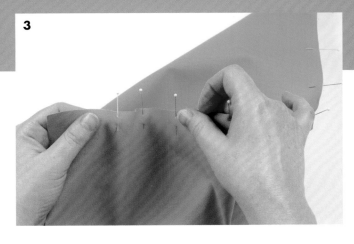

1

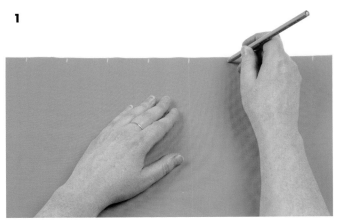

4

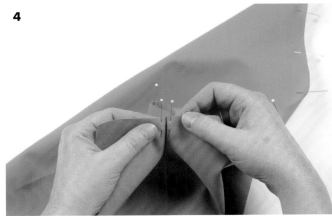

2

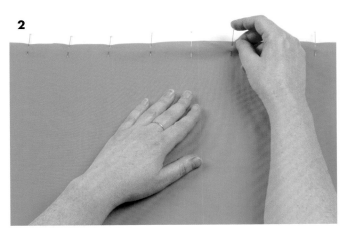

5

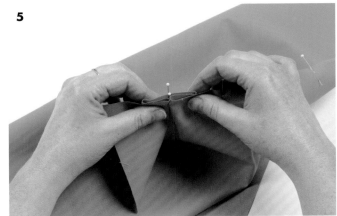

1. Following the pattern's pleat markings, use a water-soluble chalk and mark each fold.

2. Insert a pin into each mark, leaving the heads of the pins above the fabric so you can see them for folding in step 3. Be sure to use pins that will not melt under the heat of the iron.

3. Bring the first and third pins together, lining them up and leaving the excess fabric folded in between.

4. Once the first and third pins have met, pin them together to keep the fold in place.

5. Line up the pin you inserted in step 4 with the pin behind the folds. In lining up these two pins, the excess fabric should be evenly distributed on either side of the pin behind the pleat.

(continued)

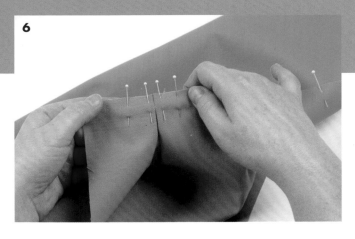

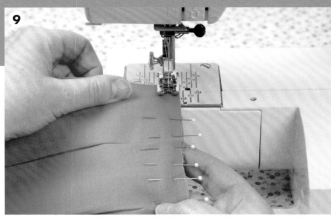

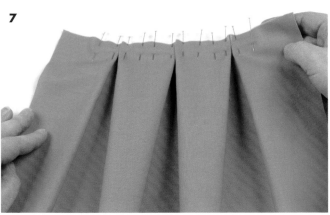

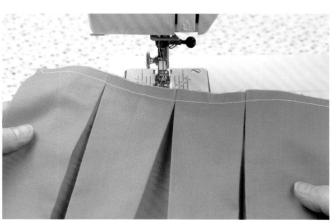

6. Insert two pins into each side of the pleat. The first pins should be immediately on either side of the folds at the center of the pleat, and the other two should be to their side, securing the folds on the other side of the pleat.

7. Continue folding and pinning around the garment until all the pleats are formed.

8. Using an iron, press the pleats, from the top of the fabric to just below the project's seam allowance, flattening the area to be sewn.

9. Baste the pleats in place with a straight stitch. Sew just within the project's seam allowance. For this example, the project calls for a ⅝" (1.5 cm) seam allowance, so I have stitched it at the ⅜" (1 cm) line.

10. Continue baste stitching across all the pleats, making sure to keep all the folds on the top and bottom of the fabric in place. After stitching, press with an iron again and sew into the seam.

BOX PLEATS

To the naked eye, box pleats can look a lot like inverted pleats, but the main difference is that unlike in an inverted pleat, the excess fabric between the center folds is on the right side of the garment instead of on the inside of the garment. Inverted pleats and box pleats are formed in almost the exact same way, just with the opposite end result.

1. Using water-soluble chalk, make pleat marks according to your pattern's markings and instructions.

2. Insert a pin into each of the pleat marks, leaving the head of the pin visible above the fabric to use as a guide in step 3. Be sure to use pins that will not melt under the heat of the iron.

3. Pull the second pin forward toward you, forming a fold. Align the first and third pins behind the second pin. Pin through the layers of the fabric where the first and third pins meet.

4. Line up the second pin with the pin behind you inserted in step 3, forming a fold on either side of it, both equidistant from the pin center point.

(continued)

1

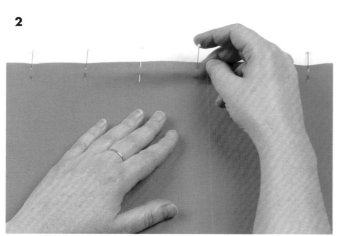

2

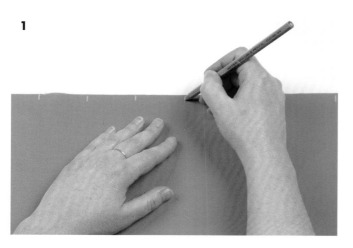

3

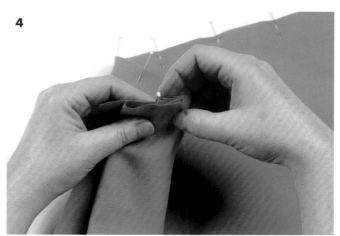

4

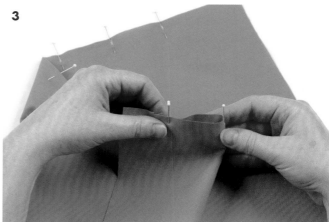

5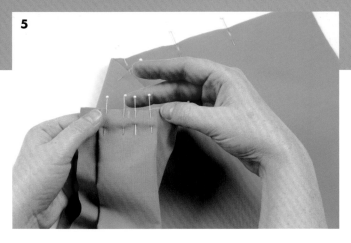

8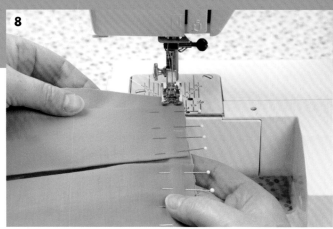

6

9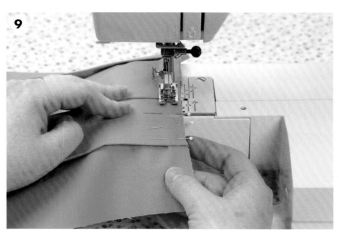

7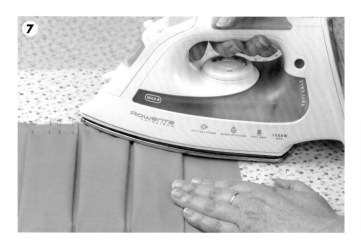

5. Insert two pins on either side of the center pin, securing the front fold of fabric as well as the fold behind. Remove the center pin.

6. Continue folding and pinning the pleats for the remainder of the garment.

7. Using an iron, press the pleats from the top of the fabric to just below the project's seam allowance.

8. Sew the pleats in place with a baste stitch. Stitch just within the project's seam allowance. In this example, the project calls for a ⅝" (1.5 cm) seam allowance and I am stitching on the ⅜" (1 cm) line.

9. Continue stitching along the pleats with a baste stitch, being careful to keep all the folds in place on the top and bottom layers of the fabric.

STITCHED DOWN PLEATS

Any pleat can be topstitched to create a smooth area prior to releasing the fullness of the pleating. The pleats can be stitched on the fold or on either side of the fold. This is commonly found in skirts to create a flattering smooth area around the waist, releasing the pleats at the hip. For this example, I am using knife pleats with a single stitch down the pleat fold.

1. After completing the pleating, pin the pleats in place from the top of the fabric to a few inches below where the stitching will end.

2. Use a seam gauge and water-soluble pencil or pen to measure down each pleat so each one begins and ends at the same spot.

3. Sew down each pleat from the top of the fabric to the mark made in step 2. Be sure to backstitch at the bottom to secure the stitch. An alternative choice to just ending at the mark is to pivot at the end of the stitching, turning toward the pleat to create a small line connecting the stitching to the pleat fold.

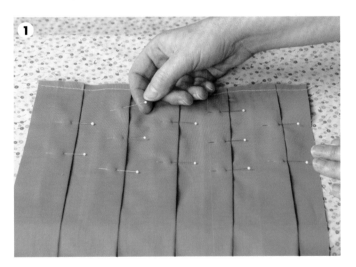

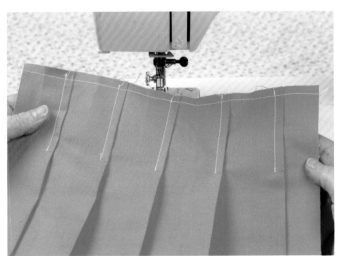

Pin Tucks

Much like pleats, pin tucks are folds made in the fabric, though unlike pleats, tucks are always stitched entirely from top to bottom on the right side of the garment. They are often found on the front of dresses and blouses. The width of the tuck as well as the space between tucks can vary from pattern to pattern. They can be spaced apart or sometimes close enough to overlap. The markings

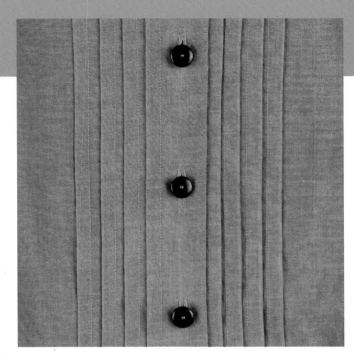

consist of a folding line and a stitching line, both of which will be transferred to the fabric. Follow your pattern's markings to make sure you are folding the correct amount so the piece with the tucks will fit the surrounding pattern pieces.

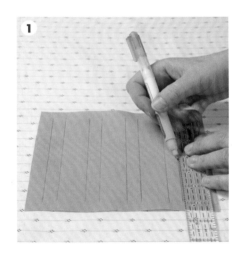

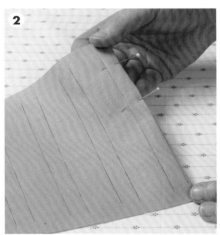

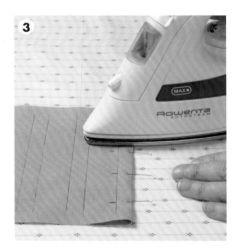

1. Use a water-soluble marking tool to transfer the markings from the pattern to the right side of the fabric. For this example, I transferred the marks by making a small dot at the top and bottom of each line before removing the pattern piece, then connected the dots with a ruler and drew a line.

2. Fold along the folding line, placing wrong sides together, and pin in place for sewing. Use glass-head pins so they will not melt under the heat of an iron.

3. Press on the fold with an iron. Read the instructions on the water-soluble marking tool used, as some are not removable after being set with an iron.

4

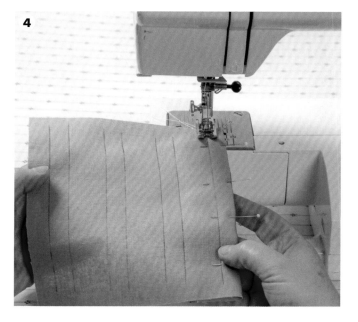

6

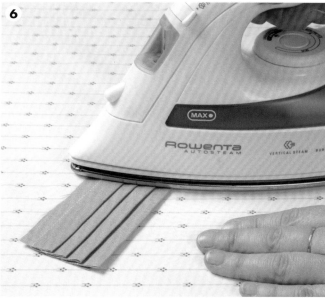

5

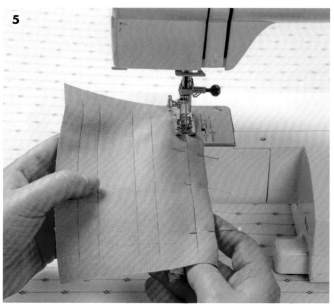

7

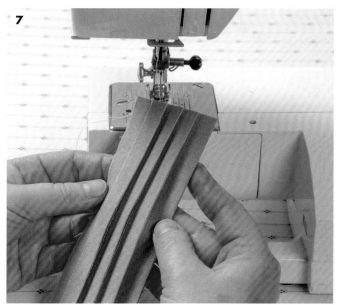

4. Stitch along the sewing line on the right side of the garment. While sewing along the line, the underside of fabric is being sewn as well.

5. Repeat steps 2 and 3 on the next tuck and sew in place. Be sure to catch the fold underneath, but not the previously sewn tuck.

6. Press the finished tucks with an iron, be sure to remove the markings from step 1 beforehand.

7. Before inserting the finished piece into the neighboring seam, sew a baste stitch inside the seam allowance at the top and bottom of the tucks to hold them in place.

Elastic Shirring

When elastic thread is sewn onto fabric, it gathers up the fabric and makes the seam stretchy, making this an ideal technique for waistbands on pants and skirts as well as for creating waist definition on a loosely designed dress. It is a simple yet effective technique that can completely transform a garment. It is best used on medium- and lightweight woven fabrics, as heavy-weight fabrics will be too bulky to gather up with the elastic thread.

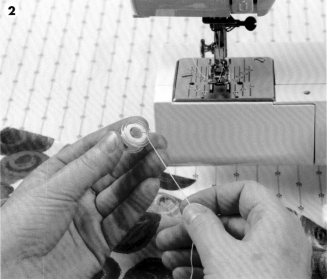

1. Using the markings on your pattern, draw on the right side of the garment a series of lines to follow for sewing the elastic shirring stitches. For this example, I simply made a dot at either side of the line and connected them with a ruler. Be sure to use a water-soluble marking tool because this is the right side of the fabric.

2. Gently wind elastic thread evenly onto an empty bobbin, until it is nearly full. Wind the thread onto the bobbin without stretching it, and move from top to bottom on the bobbin so it is evenly distributed. Place the bobbin into the sewing machine as you would normally, inserting it into the tension and pulling it up under the presser foot. The upper thread should be regular thread, and will be visible on the right side of the garment.

3. Do not backstitch at the beginning or end of the stitching, but do leave some extra thread and elastic on either side for securing afterward. Increase the stitch length a little and check using a scrap piece of fabric to confirm that the length and tension are set correctly before stitching on the final project.

4. Sew along each line, keeping the fabric flat and smooth as you stitch through it. There is no need to pull or stretch the fabric as you sew; simply make sure the gathers are not pinched as you sew.

5. Continue along all the lines of the shirring. As you sew, the fabric will gather up because of the elastic thread. When all the rows are stitched, pull the elastic and top threads to the underside of the fabric and knot in place. If you will sew the shirring into another seam, this can be skipped as the threads will be secured by the stitching of the seam.

6. Once all the rows are stitched, turn on your iron to a high steam setting and fill with water. When it is hot and steaming heavily, hover the iron over the fabric, without actually touching it, and push the steam button to release hot steam all over the threads. Move the iron around to evenly distribute the steam. The area with the stitching will reduce significantly with the use of the steam.

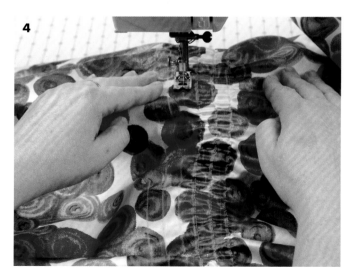

Princess Seams

A princess seam is usually found in place of darts on the front and back of a woman's dress or blouse. The bulk of the fabric that is folded in a dart is instead distributed along a curved seam that starts around the armhole or sleeve and ends at the hem of the top or dress, or at the waist if sewn into a skirt. It can be a flattering and soft approach to making curves around the body. The hardest part of sewing a princess seam is working with the excess fabric on the wider part of the curve and easing it into the seam without forming any puckers or gathers. The end result of a perfectly sewn princess seam is a smooth, pucker-free seam that flatters the body.

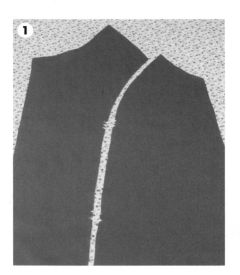

1. Cut the pattern pieces for the project you are sewing, taking extra care to clip all the marked notches along the seam. Typically, a princess seam has notches above and below the deepest part of the curve to indicate where things should line up.

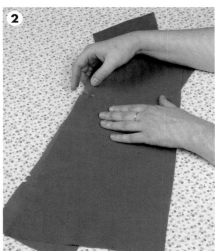

2. Place the pattern pieces with right sides together and pin at the upper notch.

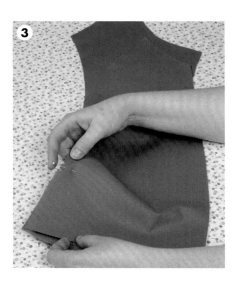

3. Pin at the lower notch, just as you did at the upper notch. If the seam is longer and contains additional notches, pin at the remaining notches.

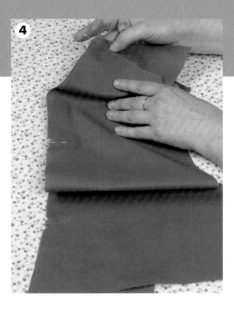

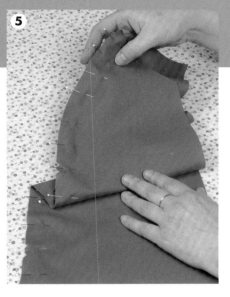

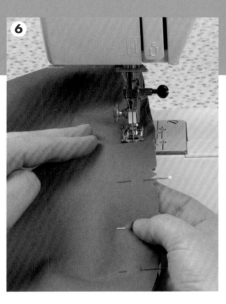

4. Pin at the top and bottom of the princess seam.

5. Pin along the remaining parts of the seam, between all the notches. At the widest part of the curve, ease the fabric to fit by placing a pressing ham

under the fabric to fill the negative space. Push all excess fabric into the body of the garment and the seam allowance, keeping the stitch line smooth. If the bulk is too great, clip into the seam allowance to release the bulk in the seam allowance.

6. Sew along the seam, keeping the stitch line smooth. Continue to push the excess fabric to the right or left of the stitch line, making sure to keep the raw edges together in the seam allowance.

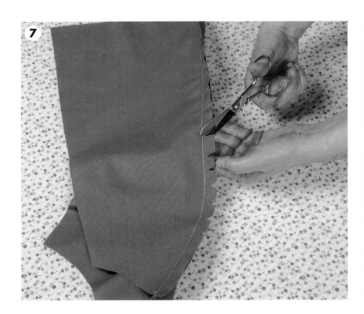

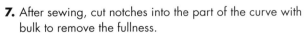

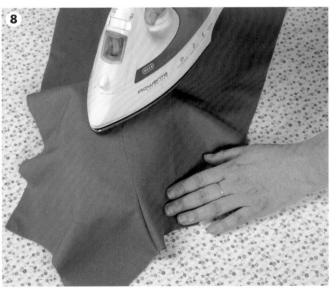

7. After sewing, cut notches into the part of the curve with bulk to remove the fullness.

8. Fold the fabric as you sewed it, wrong sides together, and press the seam using a pressing ham to assist with the curve. Open the seam and press wrong side up, pressing the seam allowance according to the pattern. Flip the piece over and press on the right side, taking care to press using a setting appropriate to the type of fabric.

Basic Waistband

Simple waistbands can be found at the top of skirts as well as pants without fly zippers. There are millions of ways to finish them, but the technique illustrated here is a great classic approach that will leave you with a professional finish that can be applied to many projects, even those that call for other finishing. For this example, I am making a simple skirt with an invisible zipper and waistband.

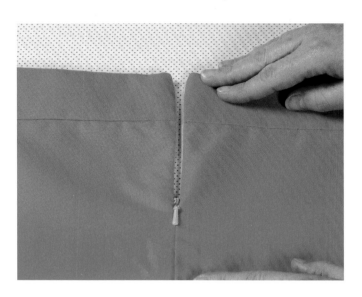

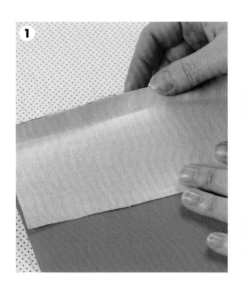

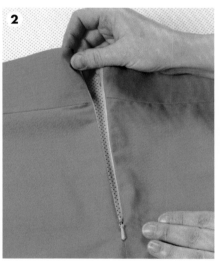

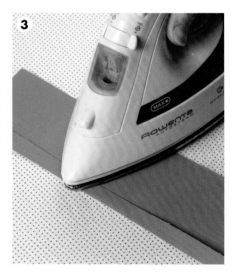

1. The outer layer of a waistband should have interfacing for stability and support. Once fused, sew the outer waistband piece to the lower skirt piece, right sides together.

2. Following the instructions for the type of zipper you plan to insert, sew the zipper into the seam of the garment.

3. Press the lower edge of the inside waistband piece, wrong sides together. This will be hand sewn to the seam allowance of the waistband, so press it the same amount as the project's seam allowance. For example if the project calls for a $5/8$" (1.5 cm) seam allowance, press up the lower edge $5/8$" (1.5 cm) to match the front waistband.

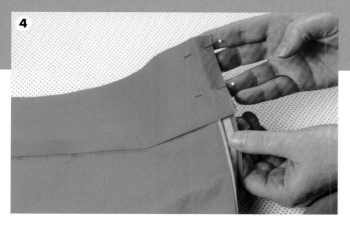

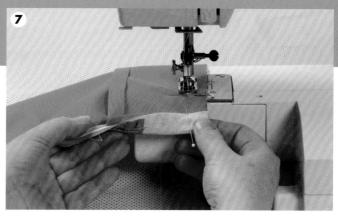

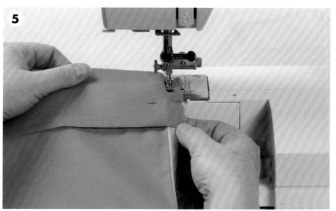

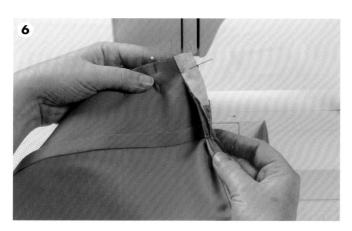

4. Pin the inner waistband piece to the garment, right sides together, along the zipper. Be sure to line up the upper waistband edge.

5. Sew along the zipper with a zipper foot, placing your stitching on the zipper tape, close to the zipper teeth.

6. Pin along the upper edge of the waistband, all around the garment. At the zipper, fold the entire edge along the zipper into the garment and pin in place.

7. Sew along the waistband at the project's seam allowance, going over all the folded layers near the zipper. Be sure to backstitch when you reach the folded end.

8. Clip the corner of the opening to the zipper to reduce bulk.

9. Use a point turner to carefully poke out the corner, exposing the zipper teeth. Press the upper edge of the waistband for a crisp seam, then finish by hand stitching the lower edge of the inner waistband to the seam allowance of the outer waistband.

In-Seam Pockets

Pockets make most things better in my opinion. An in-seam pocket is one that is sewn into the side seam of a dress, tunic, skirt, or pants. If sewn correctly, you do not see them in the finished garment. Even if the pattern did not include pockets in the plan, they are easy to add into any side seam. Using a pocket piece from another project, follow these steps to include a pocket in your next garment.

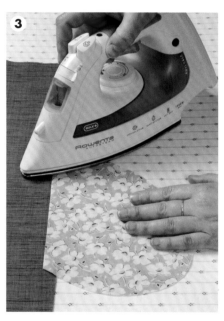

1. For each pocket, you will need two pocket pieces, as well as a front and back of the item it is going into. For my example, the garment getting pockets is a skirt. The pocket pieces should be mirror images, with one for the front and one for the back. Pin one pocket piece to the garment, right sides together. The pattern will include a notch on both the front and the back piece as well as on the pockets to use for lining up all the pieces.

2. Sew the pocket to the garment, a scant amount less than your pattern's seam allowance. If the project is sewn at a ⅝" (1.5 cm) seam allowance, then the pockets should be sewn on 1/16" (1.6 mm) less.

3. Press the pocket open, making the pocket and piece it was sewn to one unit. Repeat steps 2 and 3 on the matching pieces.

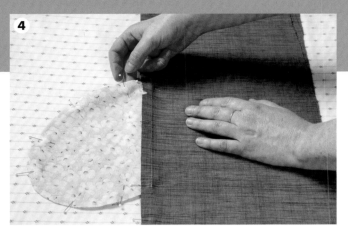

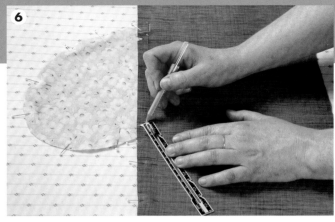

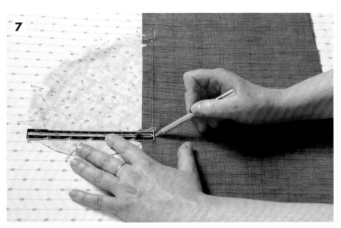

4. Place the garment right sides together and pin in place. Pin all the way around the pocket and the remaining seam above and below the pocket.

5. When sewing around the pocket, at the point where the pocket and the skirt pieces join, the seam allowance markings on the machine will be covered by the fabric. To follow along the proper seam allowance, use a chalk pencil and seam gauge to continue the line to use when sewing. Set the seam gauge to the project's seam allowance and mark along the pocket's lower edge, on the pocket, just inside the intersection of the pieces.

6. Continue the line onto the skirt piece to follow for pivoting.

7. Line up the seam gauge on the edge of the skirt piece and draw a line starting at the line from the pocket down past the intersection until you are able to see the seam allowance marking on the machine.

8. Repeat at the top of the pocket. Your lines should fall just inside the stitching that was used to attach the pocket because that was sewn at a scant seam allowance. If the seam stitch falls on or outside the stitching, the pocket stitching will be visible on the right side of the garment.

(continued)

9. Sew the skirt pieces together at the pattern's seam allowance. Once the pocket covers the machine's markings, rely on your pencil line to stay on track.

10. Pivot on the chalk line at the intersection of the pocket and the skirt.

11. Follow the pencil line onto the pocket piece, then once the machine seam allowance markings are visible, use those as your guide.

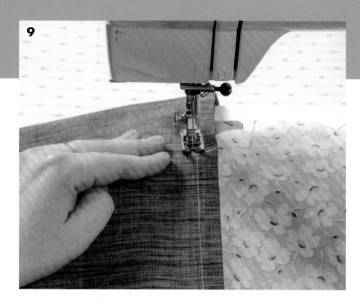

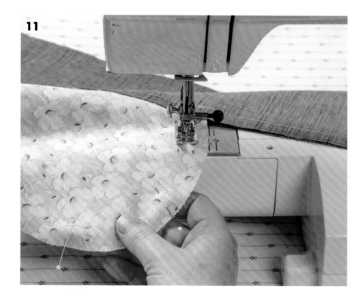

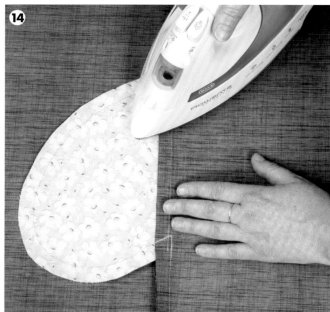

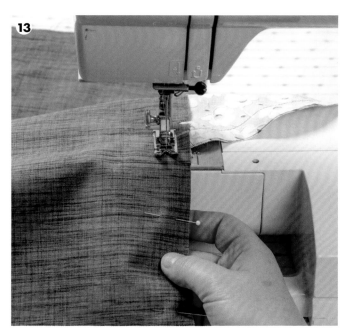

12. Repeat the pivoting and follow your chalk lines on the other end of the pocket.

13. Continue in the same stitch to finish sewing the rest of the side seam of the garment.

14. Open up the side seam, wrong side up, and press the pocket and side seam allowances toward the front.

15. Press on the right side of the seam, smoothing out the spot just at the top and bottom of the pocket. Check to make sure all the stitching from attaching the pocket is hidden.

Bias Finishing

Using bias binding to finish a raw edge is simple and effective. This can be done on necklines in place of a facing, on sleeve openings for sleeveless finishing, and even on hems if so desired. There are two common ways to apply bias binding, one that ends up being a single layer and one that is doubled over. Consider the weight and opacity of your fabric when choosing your preferred method. The double fold method might be a little easier, but both methods result in a similar appearance.

SINGLE FOLD METHOD

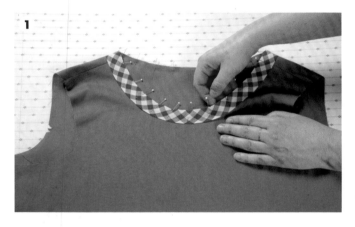

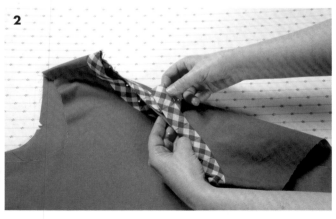

1. For this application, the bias strip should be longer than the opening and 1" (2.5 cm) wide. This should have been cut on the 45-degree true bias. Before pinning pre-packaged bias tape to the opening, be sure to press out all folds made in the manufacturing process, taking care not to stretch or warp it. Pin the bias strip to the opening with right sides together. For this example I am using a neckline and am placing the center of the length at the center front and the excess at the center back. For a hem or an armhole opening, the start and ending can be wherever you'd like.

2. At the center back, pin the two ends together where they meet, right sides together.

3. Sew the ends together at the back where they were pinned together.

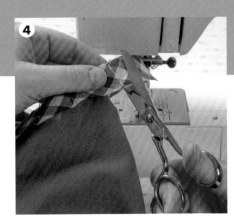

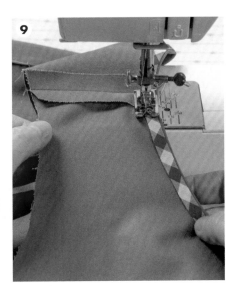

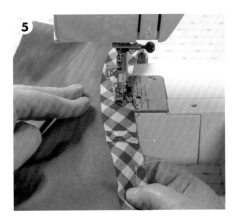

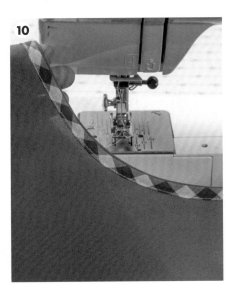

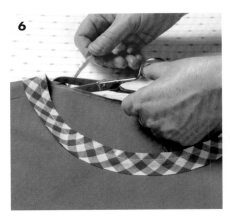

4. Trim off the extra seam allowance, leaving ¼" (6 mm) beyond the seam. Press the seam allowance open and pin it to the opening.

5. Sew the bias binding to the opening with a ¼" (6 mm) seam allowance, starting and stopping at the center back.

6. Trim the seam allowance down to ⅛" (3 mm) all the way around the opening.

7. Press the bias tape into the opening, lining up the raw edge of the binding with the stitching in step 5.

8. Press the binding into the opening a second time, this time rolling the seam just to the inside to make it invisible. Pin it in place for sewing.

9. Sew as close as you can to the inside fold of the bias binding, keeping in mind that the bobbin thread is visible on the right side of your garment.

10. Give the entire opening a final press to set the stitches and to press the bias flat.

DOUBLE FOLD METHOD

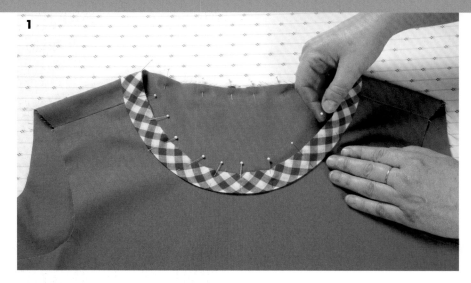

1. For a double fold version of bias binding, start with a strip that is longer than your opening and 2" (5.1 cm) wide. This should have been cut on the 45-degree true bias. Before pinning pre-packaged bias tape to the opening, be sure to press out all folds made in the manufacturing process, taking care not to stretch or warp it. Fold the 2" (5.1 cm) bias strip in half lengthwise, wrong sides together, making it 1" (2.5 cm) wide, right sides out. Pin the bias strip to the opening with right sides together. For this example I am using a neckline and am placing the center of the length at the center front and the excess at the center back. For a hem or an armhole opening, the start and ending can be where you desire.

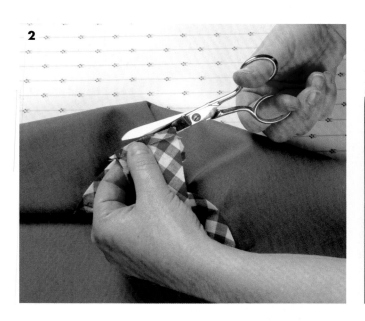

2. Open up the fold at the center back and pin the ends together where they meet at the center back. Stitch the ends together where pinned, right sides facing. Trim off the extra seam allowance, leaving ¼" (6 mm) of fabric beyond the seam.

3. Press the seam allowance open where the center back was sewn together.

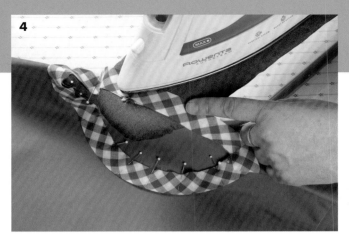

4

7

5

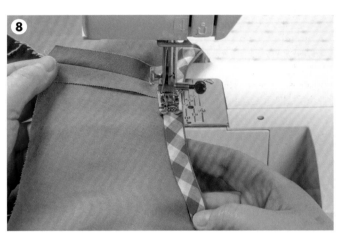

8

6

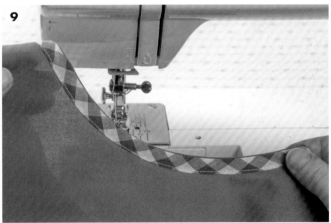

9

4. Repress the original fold in the bias binding and pin to the opening.

5. Sew the bias binding to the opening using a ½" (1.3 cm) seam allowance, starting and stopping at the joined seam.

6. Trim the seam allowance to ⅛" (3 mm) all the way around the opening.

7. Fold the entire bias binding into the opening, rolling the seam into the inside of the garment so it cannot be seen from the right side.

8. Stitch the binding as close as you can to the inside fold, keeping in mind that the stitch is visible on the right side of the garment.

9. Press the entire opening to set the stitches and to press the bias binding flat.

Collars

Adding a flat or rolled collar to any blouse or dress brings in a great touch of interest and personal style. I love topping nearly everything I make with a flat Peter Pan collar. Rolled collars are a bit trickier to add, but there is tremendous reward when the work is put into a great collar, as nothing elevates a handmade garment like a beautifully sewn collar.

FLAT COLLARS

A flat collar is a shape that is added to the neckline of a garment. The opening with the collar added is then finished, including the collar in the seam. It is the easiest collar to make and can come in nearly every shape and size desired. For this example I am making a classic flat, Peter Pan–style collar.

1. Cut two collar pieces. Some patterns will come with an under collar and an upper collar. If this is the case, the upper collar, which will be visible on top, is slightly larger than the under collar, which will be underneath, and the sewn seam will naturally roll to the underside. Cut a piece of woven fusible interfacing to match the upper collar. Press the interfacing to the upper collar, then pin the two collar pieces together, right sides facing.

2. Sew from one front corner around to the other corner, following the pattern's seam allowance.

3

4

5

6

7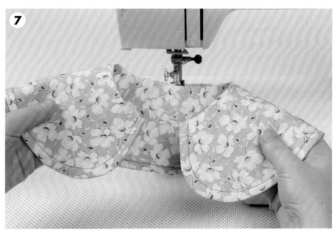

3. When sewing around tight curves, reduce your stitch length to sew shorter stitches for a more precise and fluid curve. For a flat collar, do not sew the inner curve that will go around the neck, as this opening is where the collar will be turned right side out and attached to the pattern.

4. Trim the seam allowance down to ¼" (6 mm) all the way around the sewn edges of the collar. If the collar has an angled corner, trim off the tip of the corner at a right angle. Do not trim the area that was not sewn.

5. Turn the collar right-side out and press the seam flat with an iron.

6. Topstitching is usually an optional choice for collars. If you choose to topstitch, try using a quarter-inch foot for precision stitching. Sew from one front corner to the other corner. If your collar has a right angle, mark the pivot point with a water-soluble pencil or pen before sewing.

7. After topstitching, give the entire collar a final press and follow the pattern's instructions to add it to your project's neckline.

ROLLED COLLARS

Unlike a flat collar, a rolled collar attaches to the neckline, then lifts up along the neck and folds out onto the body. Because of this, the collar needs to be steamed and shaped to give the fabric memory so it will keep its shape. Like flat collars, rolled collars also come in a wide range of shapes and sizes.

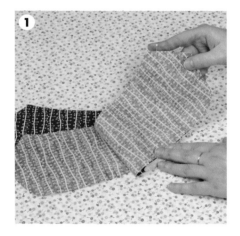

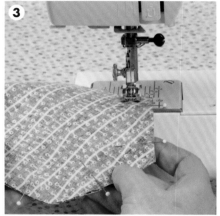

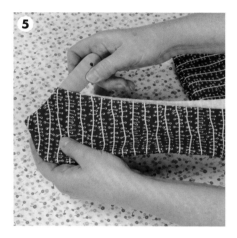

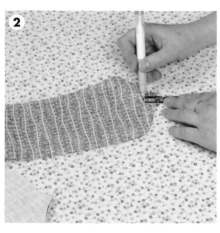

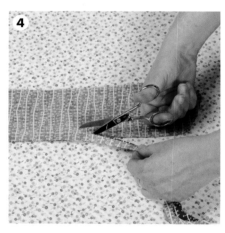

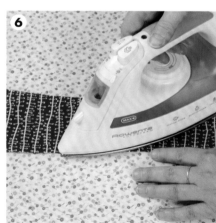

1. Cut the upper and under collar pieces from your fabric and one upper collar piece from woven fusible interfacing. With an iron, press the interfacing to the upper collar. Pin the upper and under collar pieces together, right sides facing.

2. If your collar has corners, mark the pivot points with a chalk pencil and seam gauge according to the project's seam allowance.

3. Sew the upper and under collar pieces together, pivoting and curving where necessary. If there are any tight curves, reduce your stitch length for a shorter, smoother stitch. Do not sew the opening that attaches to the neckline, as this is where the collar will be turned right-side out.

4. Trim down the seam allowance to ¼" (6 mm) on the sides that were

sewn in step 3. Do not trim the areas not sewn. If there is a right angle on your collar, trim the corner tip off at a diagonal to reduce bulk.

5. Turn the collar right-side out and use a point turner to push out the seam allowance and any corners.

6. With an iron, press the entire collar flat, focusing on the sewn outer seam.

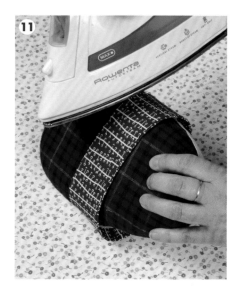

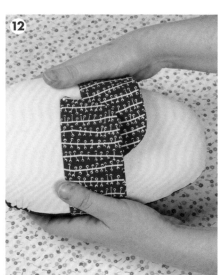

7. Fold the collar as it will be when finished, bringing the front corners forward.

8. Open up the collar and lay a pressing ham in the middle. Pin the right corner to the ham by pushing the pin directly through the collar into the ham.

9. Repeat with the other side of the collar, wrapping the left side around the ham and holding it in place with a pin.

10. Fill your iron with water and set to a hot steam setting. Once hot, heavily steam the collar. The goal is to give this shaped fabric memory.

11. Continue steaming with a hot iron around to the back of the collar.

12. While hot and damp from the steam of the iron, press the collar with your hands, molding it to the ham. Leave the collar pinned to the ham in this shape until completely dry, preferably for a few hours or overnight. Once done, continue with your pattern's instructions to attach the collar to your project.

Sleeves

No matter how long or short a sleeve's length, there are a variety of ways a sleeve can connect with the rest of the garment you are making. The most common sleeves are set-in sleeves, raglan sleeves, and shirting sleeves. Each is attached to the shoulder and side seam in a different way, and in this section all three of those are covered. For sleeveless finishing, see the section on bias finishing, which can be used to finish any opening, including an armhole.

SET-IN SLEEVE

The most common of all sleeves is the set-in sleeve, which consists of a sleeve already sewn at the side seam inserted into an armhole in the garment. The tricky part about a set-in sleeve is that in order to have ease and movement in the shoulder, the circle of the armhole needs to be smaller than the sleeve to be inserted. Therefore the sleeve must be eased into the smaller opening, and this must be done without any puckering or pleats in the shoulder seam.

1

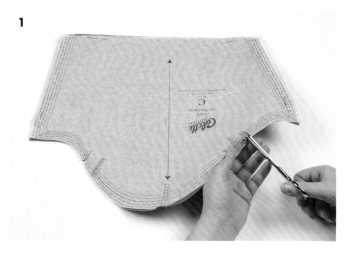

2

1. Cut two sleeves that are mirror images of each other. With the sleeve pattern piece still pinned to the sleeves, cut the notches for the front and back sides of the sleeve. Two notches always represents the back of the garment and a single notch always represents the front of the garment. This is universal throughout all patterns.

2. Peel back the pattern and use a water-soluble chalk pencil to mark the spots on the sleeve for the ease stitching and for the top of the sleeve cap.

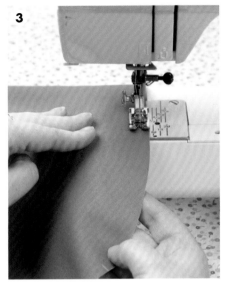

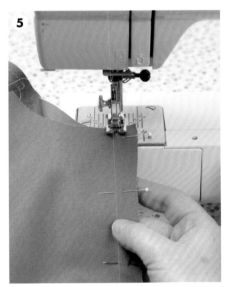

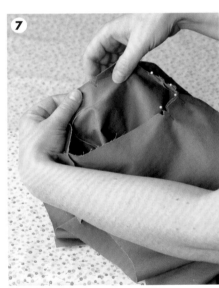

3. Using a baste stitch, sew from the two ease stitching dots on the front and back of the sleeve. For a project with a ⅝" (1.5 cm) seam allowance, use ⅜" (1 cm) seam allowance for this stitch. Leave long 2" to 3" (5.1 to 7.6 cm) thread tails at each end.

4. Repeat step 3, this time sewing on the ¾" (1.9 cm) seam allowance. This places the two baste stitches just above and below the stitch line.

5. Fold the sleeve in half, right sides together. Pin the side seam of the sleeve and sew with a straight stitch. This can be done either before or after the baste stitching, but often it is easier to do the baste stitches with the sleeve flat and open.

6. Turn the garment and armhole wrong-side out. Turn the sleeve right-side out. Drop the sleeve into the armhole opening with the hem first. Line up the double notches and pin. Continue pinning from the notches to the armhole side seam, away from the baste stitches.

7. Line up the single notches and pin. Repeat as you did in step 6 and pin to the side seam.

(continued)

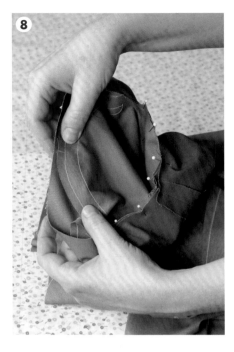

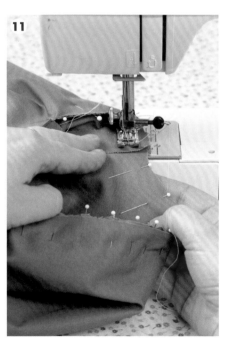

8. Line up the chalk pencil mark at the top of the sleeve cap with the armhole shoulder seam. Pin in place.

9. Separate the front and back baste threads on one side of the sleeve. Tuck the back baste threads behind the sleeve and keep the ones facing you in front. Grab the two baste threads in front and pull on them while gathering the fabric into the sleeve opening. This is how you "ease" the sleeve into the armhole. Only gather and ease one half of the sleeve, from the notch to the top of the sleeve cap pin.

10. Smooth the fabric between the notch and the sleeve cap pin until all the excess fabric is to the left or the right of the stitch line. Pin that eased section in place. Repeat the easing process on the other half of the sleeve and pin in place.

11. Starting at the sleeve side seam, stitch along the flat part of the sleeve opening.

12. Continue sewing into the eased section. Keep the raw edges together and the excess fabric to either side of the stitch line. Be careful not to sew a pinch into the seam.

13. After passing through the eased section, continue around the rest of the sleeve opening and end where you started.

14. Gently remove the baste stitches both above and below the stitch line.

15. Trim and grade the sleeve seam allowance. Turn right-side out and fit the pressing ham into the shoulder seam, filling the space for the shoulder. Press the sleeve seam allowance toward the sleeve, away from the shoulder. Mold the shoulder to the ham.

SHIRTING SLEEVE

A shirting sleeve is the type of sleeve that you would find on a classic button-down shirt style, for both men and women. This style of sleeve is sewn before the side seams are sewn, and are not "set" into the sleeve hole of the body of the shirt. This type of insertion is possible because the sleeve cap has a less severe curve. Most often a traditional shirting sleeve is sewn with a flat-fell seam. For this example, I am illustrating the insertion rather than the finishing, which can be found in the seam section of the book.

1. The front and back of the shirt should already be sewn at the shoulder seams, and the side seams of the sleeve and the shirt should not be sewn. Line up the sleeve on the shirt with right sides facing. Pin at the marking for the sleeve cap center, the start and end of the sleeve, and any other key notches in between.

2. Stitch at the project's seam allowance, starting at one end of the sleeve. Curve the two pieces to match as they move through the machine.

3. Continue around the sleeve cap, keeping the raw edges together and rotating around the sleeve. Follow the pattern's instructions for finishing the seam allowance and joining the side seams of the sleeve and body of the shirt.

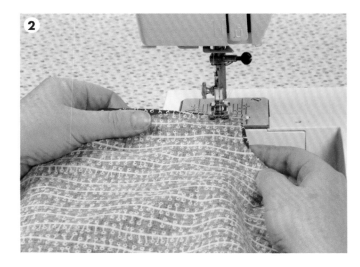

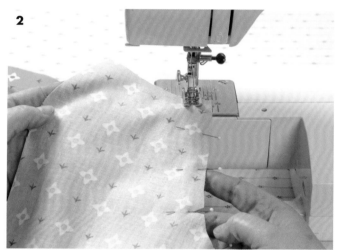

RAGLAN SLEEVE

A raglan sleeve is the easiest sleeve to put into a garment, making it an ideal sleeve for beginner projects. The sleeve is attached to the bodice front and back with a diagonal seam that reaches from under the arm to the neck. The seam is only slightly curved, but requires some pressing and shaping after being sewn.

1. The left side of this front bodice already has a raglan sleeve attached. On the right side, pin the curve of the seam, right sides together. Match the notches on the pattern first, as the curve might not line up in an intuitive manner.

2. Sew the sleeve to the bodice with the pattern's seam allowance in mind. Gently sew around the underarm curve.

3. With the wrong side facing up, press the seam with a pressing ham underneath. Depending on the severity of the curve, notching or seam grading will likely be necessary. Follow the pattern's instructions to complete the steps.

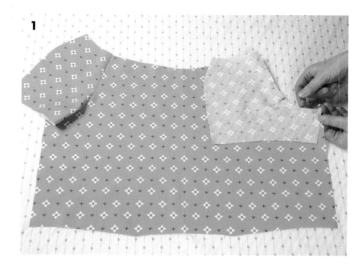

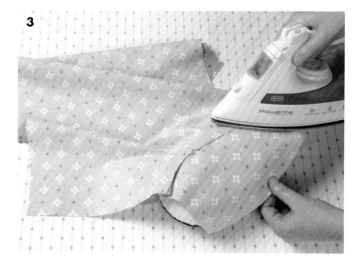

Sleeve Finishing

For as many sleeve types that exist in the world there are as many ways to finish each and every one of them. The most common sleeve finish is a simple double fold hem that is topstitched. This can be found on sleeves of all styles and lengths. In this section I will also explore finishing the sleeve with an elastic casing as well as with a cuff and placket, as found on a dress shirt. For elastic finishing without a casing, see the section about elastic gathering without a casing.

There are two main ways to handle a basic sleeve hem with a double fold topstitch finish. The first is to treat the hem of the sleeve prior to finishing the side seam of the sleeve, and the second is to treat the hem in its entirety after sewing the side seam of the sleeve. Either can be used for most applications, depending on which method you prefer.

DOUBLE FOLD SLEEVE HEM, METHOD 1

1. With the side seam of the sleeve unsewn, lay the sleeve down, wrong-side up. Measure and pin the hem of the sleeve the amount called for in the project's sleeve hem allowance.

2. Press the fold on top of the pins, making sure they are of a variety that will not melt under the heat of the iron.

3. Fold the hem a second time and pin in place.

4. Press again with the iron. Pressing it in preparation for the hem before sewing the side seam can make forming the hem much easier.

5. Remove the pins from the hem to allow for sewing the side seam.

6. Pin the side seam and open up the folds pressed for the hem.

7. Sew the side seam of the sleeve, sewing through the pressed area while making sure it is open and flat.

8. Finish the side seam allowance and press. Fold the hem, following the previously pressed folds of the hem. Press if necessary, especially in the area around the side seam that was just sewn.

9. Re-pin the sleeve hem for sewing, working all the way around the hem.

10. Stitch the hem of the sleeve, sewing as close as possible to the inner fold, starting and ending at the sleeve's side seam to hide the backstitch. Finish the hem with a press of the iron, using a sleeve board to press it in the round.

DOUBLE FOLD HEM, METHOD TWO

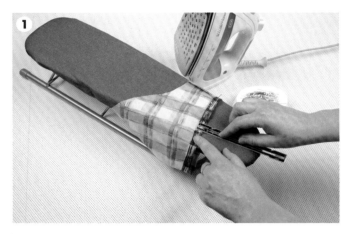

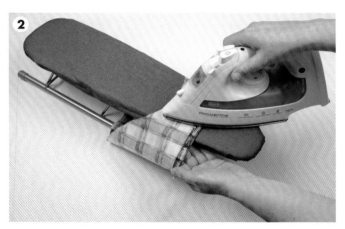

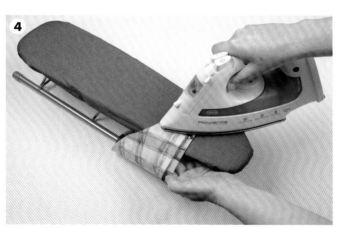

1. Your sleeve side seam should already be sewn and finished before this step. Fit the sleeve onto a sleeve board wrong-side up and fold the hem up with wrong sides together the amount indicated in the pattern instructions. Pin in place.

2. Press the fold on the pins, making sure the pins used will not melt under the heat of the iron.

3. Fold and pin the sleeve hem a second time, again following the sleeve hem allowance for your project.

4. Press the second fold with an iron.

5. Insert the sleeve into the sewing machine and sew as close as possible to the inner fold, starting and stopping at the sleeve side seam.

6. To finish the hem, slide the sleeve back onto the sleeve board and give it one final press with an iron.

ELASTIC SLEEVE HEM

If instead of a basic fold on the hem of the sleeve, you would prefer to grip it closer to the body, all that is necessary is to insert elastic into the hem. This is especially nice on feminine garments and children's wear.

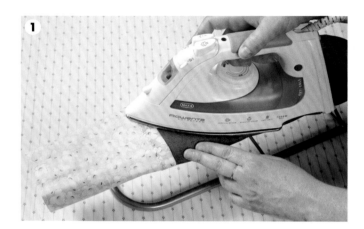

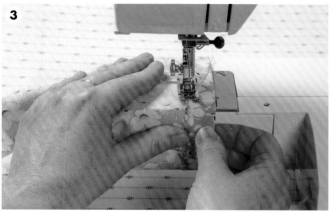

1. The side seam of the sleeve should already be sewn before starting this step. In addition, the lower hem of the sleeve should be finished with your choice of finishing stitch. Insert the sleeve onto the sleeve board wrong-side up and press the sleeve hem allowance up, wrong sides together.

2. Pin the sleeve hem in place for sewing.

3. Insert the sleeve into the sewing machine. Start sewing the sleeve hem, stitching as close to the inner edge of the sleeve hem as possible. Begin stitching near the sleeve side seam. When coming around with the stitch, stop about 1" (2.5 cm) before reaching the start of the stitch. Be sure to backstitch at the start and end of this stitch.

4. Fold the end of the elastic and secure to a bodkin. Insert the bodkin into the opening left in the sleeve hem and feed the elastic around the sleeve.

5. The elastic will be shorter in length than the sleeve hem, so as the elastic is being fed into the opening, pin the end of the elastic not attached to the bodkin to prevent it from being pulled into the casing.

6. When the bodkin has gone all the way around, pull the bodkin and elastic out of the opening.

7. Overlap the two ends of the elastic and pin in place.

8. Insert the elastic into the sewing machine and sew a zigzag stitch back and forth a couple of times. This zigzag stitch is flexible, so it will stretch with the elastic.

9. Pin the opening in the sleeve hem closed and stitch. Start and end in line with your previous stitching.

Sleeve Cuff and Placket

If you have ever seen a dress shirt, it is likely you have seen a cuff and placket. A placket is a finished slit that allows the sleeve hem to open and close, and the cuff is the wide band that finishes off the shirt sleeve and placket. Nearly every button-down shirt has some variation of this finishing. There are as many ways to sew a cuff and placket as there are styles of shirts. For my personal sewing, this is the method I use and find the most effective.

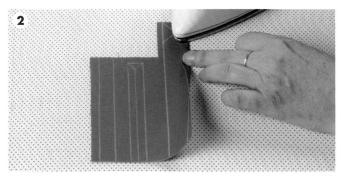

1. Cut two placket pieces, one for each sleeve. Place wrong-side up, and transfer all the placket markings to the fabric.

2. Press the far right side and the far left side into the piece, wrong sides together. Snip at the inner corner and fold the small upper left piece into the fabric. Form the triangle at the top right by folding the right side down along the diagonal, followed by the left side. Press during each fold.

3. Form any pleats or gathers in the sleeve hem prior to pinning the placket to it. Check with the pattern's instructions to see if either are required. Line up the placket placement with the pattern markings, and pin the placket to the shirt sleeve with the right side of the placket on the wrong side of the sleeve. Stitch around the long rectangle drawn into the placket.

4. Cut down the center of the rectangle sewn in step 3, stopping short of the end and following the markings to cut toward each upper corner.

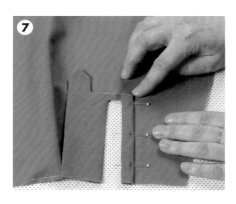

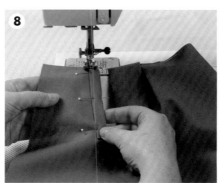

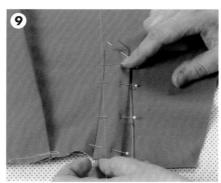

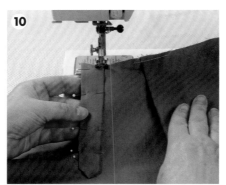

5. Turn the sleeve over and pull the placket through the slit you just cut in step 4.

6. Press the placket flat on the right side of the sleeve.

7. Fold the raw edge of the right side of the placket, tucking the raw edge under the fold. Pin in place, and press with an iron to flatten before sewing.

8. Stitch the fold, sewing close to the fold made in step 7.

9. Pick up the left side of the placket and fold it to the right. Pull it over the opening so that the right edge lines up with the recently sewn right edge from step eight. Pin in place.

10. Stitch along the outer edge of the pointed piece, pivoting at each of the corners at the top. Follow the pattern markings to pivot below the last corner to sew across the piece, lining up with the first row of stitches. If you've not done so already, sew the side seam of the sleeve together and finish the seam edge as desired.

11. Prepare two cuffs by pressing interfacing to them and stitching them together along the right curve, lower edge, and left curve. Fold one edge of the cuff down and baste. This amount will vary based on your pattern's seam allowance but will be in the ¼" to ³/₈" (6 mm to 1 cm) range. Pin the cuff to the sleeve with the longer edge on top and the shorter basted edge underneath. Stitch along this edge. Trim the seam allowance and turn the cuff right-side out, press well, and topstitch to finish. Follow the pattern markings for buttonhole and button placement.

Anatomy of a Garment

Understitching (1)	Bust darts (6)
Seam grading (2)	Waist darts (7)
Invisible zipper (3)	Gathering (8)
Set-in sleeves (4)	In-seam pockets (9)
Double fold sleeve hem (5)	Hand stitched hem (10

Directional print (1)	Waist darts (6)
Invisible zipper (2)	Topstitching (7)
Understitching (3)	Gathering (8)
Bias sleeveless binding (4)	In-seam pockets (9)
Bust darts (5)	Hand stitched hem (10)

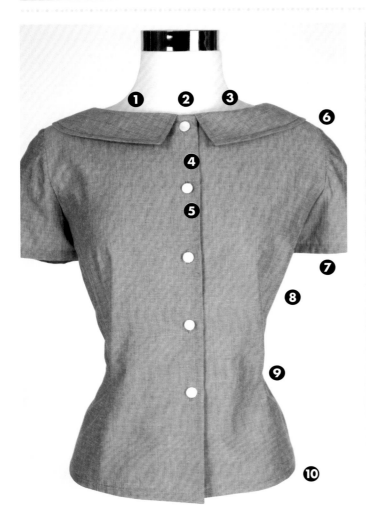

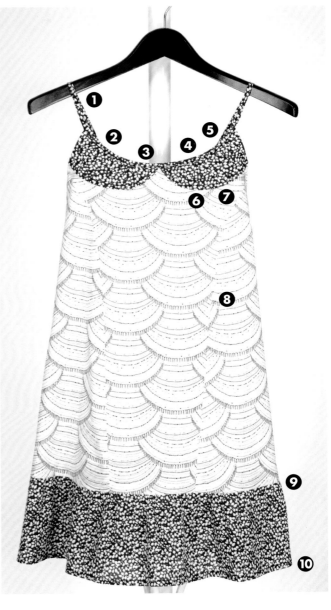

Flat collar (1)

Seam grading (2)

Understitching (3)

Buttonholes (4)

Shank buttons (5)

Set-in sleeves (6)

Double fold sleeve hem (7)

Bust darts (8)

Release pleats (9)

Double fold shirt hem (10)

Bias binding (1)

Neckline facings (2)

Seam grading (3)

Understitching (4)

Flat collar (5)

Clipping curves (6)

Topstitching (7)

Princess seams (8)

Gathering (9)

Double fold hem (10)

FINISHING TOUCHES

You have measured, cut, sewn, and assembled your newest creation, and now it is time to finish it off. This can be the most satisfying part of any project, as the end draws near and the garment is almost ready to be worn or given as a gift to a loved one. In this chapter we will talk about all kinds of hems and a few other finishing details to consider.

Patch Pockets

Unlike an inseam pocket that is included during the construction of the garment, a patch pocket is attached to the outside of the garment, often after the item is completed. Note that sometimes it is easier to attach patch pockets before finishing all the construction, so if you know you want to include them, it can be done earlier in the process. But if you decide you'd like to add patch pockets once a garment is complete, that is usually possible as well.

1. Cut the size and shape of the patch pocket you want to add. Nearly any shape can be sewn onto a garment, but for my example I am using a small pointed bottom pocket, commonly found on the chest of a blouse or larger on the back of pants. Fold the top edge down once and press, with wrong sides together. Fold a second time to hide the raw edge and press again.

2. Press in each side of the pocket, wrong sides together.

3. Open up all the folds except for the double fold at the top of the pocket. Stitch the fold in place. I used a quarter-inch seam foot for this step.

4. Re-press all the folds as well as the edge sewn in step 3. Pin in place on the project. Though the top edge will not be sewn, pin the top edge down for extra security when stitching.

5. Measure with a seam gauge and use a water-soluble pen or pencil to mark all pivot points around the entire pocket.

6. Start at the top right corner and backstitch to secure. Continue around the pocket.

7. Pivot at each corner, being sure to sink the needle into the exact mark made in step 5, then lifting the presser foot and pivoting. Lower the foot and continue on to the next corner.

8. Backstitch at the end and press with an iron. If desired, stitch a second row of topstitching close to the edge of the pocket for a traditional double stitch look.

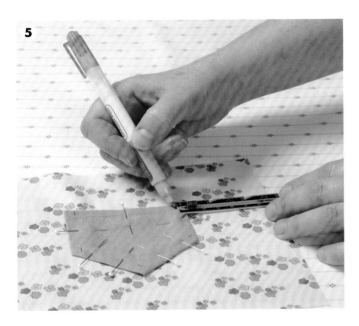

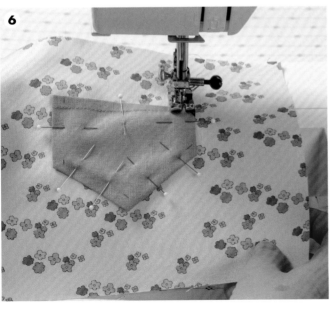

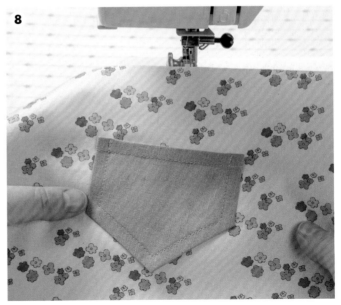

Hems

The choice of how to hem a garment is often decided by the style of the item and the fabric you are using. For thick fabrics, folding a double fold hem would be too bulky. For nicer dresses, topstitching would look too casual. So take some time to decide what is appropriate for the project you are working on. This is an area where it is common to veer from the pattern's instructions, because the hem is typically last. Do take into account, however, the hem allowance for the project, as that will tell you how much you have to work with to achieve the designer's chosen length. In this section, I will show examples of many sewing machine techniques. For hand sewing choices, see the earlier section of the book on hand sewing stitches.

SINGLE FOLD HEM

A single fold hem is exactly as it sounds: fabric that has been folded one single time, wrong sides together, into the underside of the garment. If this method is chosen, consider how to finish the raw edge of the fabric, because it will be exposed if the underside of the garment is ever seen. In the steps that follow, the fabric edge is finished with a 3-step zigzag stitch.

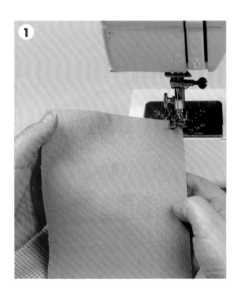

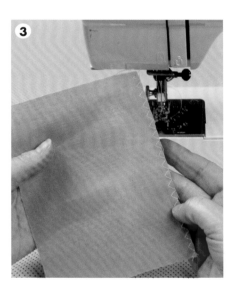

1. Insert the hem into the machine to finish as desired. For a 3-step zigzag finish on the edge, stitch with a ⅛" (3 mm) seam allowance.

2. Stitch until reaching the end of the hem's raw edge.

3. Press the edge to set the stitches and smooth out the fabric before hemming.

4. Fold the hem up into the garment, wrong sides together, and pin in place. Be sure to use pins that can withstand the heat of the iron without melting.

5. Press with an iron.

6. Insert the fabric into the sewing machine and stitch with a straight stitch close to the top raw edge of the fabric. Sew with the wrong side facing you so you can see where the stitching is in relation to the fold.

7. Continue sewing all the way around the garment. For this example, I am only sewing a small piece, but for a garment, you would sew to the end of the other side or meet back up with the beginning stitches.

8. Taking into account the type of fabric, press the hem and stitches with an iron.

DOUBLE FOLD HEM

A double fold hem can be folded two equal amounts, or it can be folded a small amount first, followed by a larger fold. Take into account the weight and opacity of the fabric before choosing one option over the other.

1. Fold the first fold, wrong sides together, and pin in place.

2. Press the fold with an iron.

3. Fold a second time and pin in place. Again, this can be an equal amount to the first fold, or the second fold can be larger.

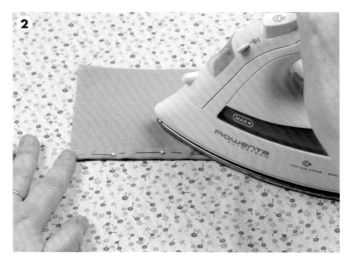

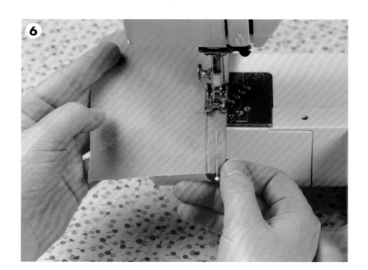

4. Press the second fold with an iron.

5. Insert the fabric into the machine and sew close to the inner fold. Stitch with the wrong side facing you so you are able to see where the stitch is landing on the fold.

6. Continue sewing until you have reached the other end of the hem or have sewn in a circle back to the beginning.

7. Finish the hem with a press of the iron to set the stitches and make the bottom hem fold crisp.

MACHINE-SEWN BLIND STITCH HEM

If you desire an invisible hem, but do not want to take the time to stitch it by hand, the machine-sewn blind stitch hem is a great choice. It can take a little practice to get the hang of this hem, and your machine's manual will likely have some instruction to assist you, so practice it on scraps first before sewing on your final garment.

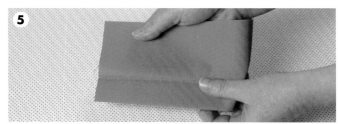

1. The raw edge of the fabric folded to the wrong side will be visible, so before sewing the hem, take time to finish the edge. On my example, I used a 3-step zigzag stitch. Press up the hem, wrong sides together, to the desired hem allowance.

2. Rotate the hem and fold back the garment with right sides together to expose the raw edge of the hem.

3. Lay the piece down and lightly press on the wrong side of the garment, exposing the raw edge.

4. Replace the presser foot on your machine with a blind hem presser foot. Consult your machine's manual to see which foot is correct for your machine's make and model. The foot will likely have a slightly shorter side and a slightly longer

side. The shorter side will ride on the folded edge because it is thicker than the right side, which will have the longer side on top of it. Set the machine to the blind hem stitch. For my example, I used a stitch length of 2.0 and a stitch width of 3.0. The machine will stitch a couple of stitches on the right side, followed by a single stitch on the left, making a tiny dot of thread. Continue around the hem with this stitch.

5. When opened, a correctly sewn blind stitch hem will have only little dots showing on the right side of the garment, with all the other stitching on the fold of the hem allowance inside.

6. Iron the hem, removing any evidence of the pressing you did in step 3. Remember to set the iron according to your fabric type.

ROLLED HEM

A rolled hem is a tiny hem that looks impossibly difficult to sew, but if you follow the method I use, it is actually very easy. Perfect for lightweight and sheer fabrics, this is a tiny double fold hem. Many sewing machines have rolled hem presser feet to do the two folds for you as you sew, but I prefer to do it without the foot, as I think this leaves a better finish in the end and is no more challenging.

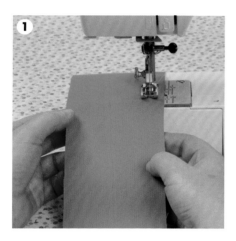

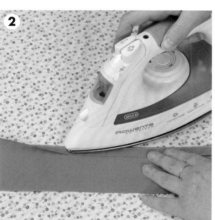

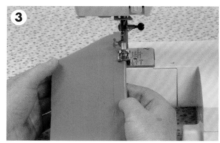

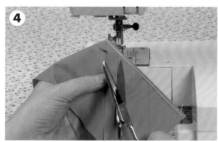

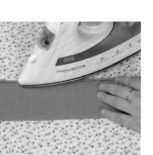

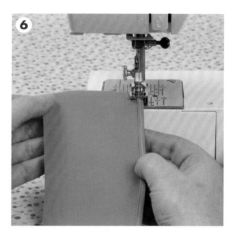

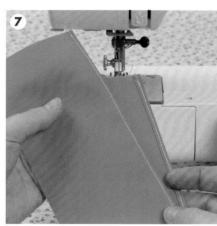

1. Using a straight stitch, sew a line along the hem, ¼" (6 mm) less than you'd like the final hem to be. So if you want a 1" (2.5 cm) hem, stitch this line at the ¾" (1.9 cm) seam allowance line.

2. Fold the fabric, wrong sides together, rolling the stitch line just to the other side of the fold.

3. Stitch directly on top of the first stitch line.

4. Trim off the extra fabric to the side of the stitching.

5. Press the stitching to the inside of the hem a second time, wrong sides together.

6. Insert the fabric into the machine and stitch again, directly on top of the previous stitching.

7. On the inside of the garment there will be two stitches, one directly on top of the other on a very small fold, and on the outside of the garment is only one stitch. Give the hem a final press.

FACED HEM

A faced hem is made by sewing a "facing" to the hem, much like you would sew a facing to the neckline of a garment. This is an ideal finish for a hem that is slightly curved, which is challenging to do perfectly due to the bulk that curves create. It is also great for a hem that is shorter than desired and doesn't have enough length to allow for a proper hem, as you only have to sacrifice the seam allowance in sewing on the facing.

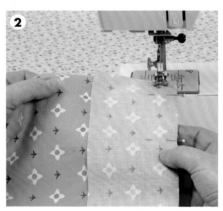

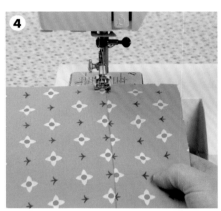

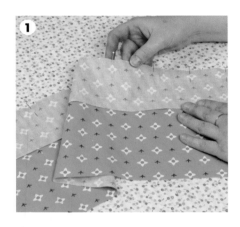

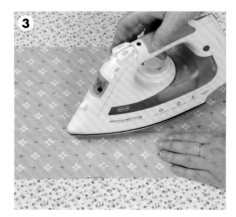

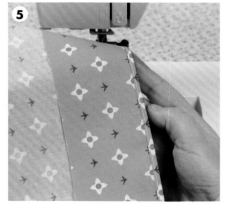

1. Pin the facing piece to the hem of the garment, right sides together.

2. Stitch the facing to the hem using the pattern's seam allowance requirement.

3. Press on the wrong side of the item on the seam, pressing the seam allowance up toward the garment and away from the facing.

4. Understitch the facing to the skirt, sewing just inside the seam.

5. Press the facing and stitch to the underside of the garment. This provides a clean seamless finish on the front and rolls the rest to the wrong side. Finish the upper edge of the facing as desired for either a topstitched or an invisible hem.

SCALLOPED HEM

Looking for something a bit different on the hem of your next project? Well, perhaps a scalloped hem is the answer. This is much like sewing a faced hem, except that the hem and facing have scallops cut into them. The trick with this hem is to take slow and steady stitches around each curve to keep them smooth and even.

1. Cut a scalloped piece to match the hem of your garment. Pin them right sides together.

2. Use a seam gauge and chalk pencil to mark an X above the point where each scallop meets. This is your pivot point.

3. Stitch along each scallop, being extra careful to be smooth and even around the curves. Reducing your stitch length can assist in more precise curves.

4. Pivot at each point by sinking the needle into the pivot mark made in step 2, then rotate the fabric, lower the presser foot, and continue sewing.

5. Trim the seam allowance down to ¼" (6 mm) very carefully around each curve.

6. At each point, clip directly into the seam allowance, getting very close to the stitching. Reduce the fabric on either side of the point by shaving away a bit more, trimming to ⅛" (3 mm) at those points.

7. Turn the garment right-side out. Use a point turner to push out the scallops. Be extra careful not to poke through the fabric.

8. Press the scallops flat with an iron. Finish the top of the scallop facing as desired.

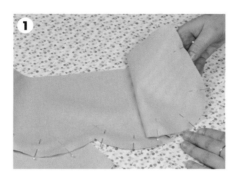

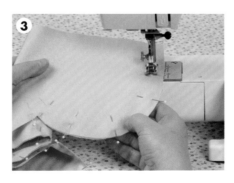

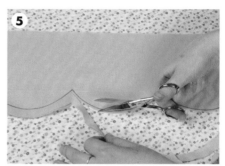

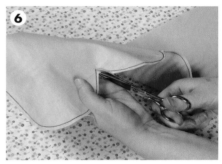

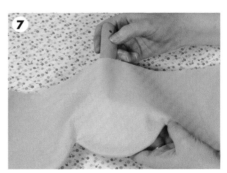

Sash Belt

Many projects call for a fabric belt tie, which is a nice way to cinch in a waist on a full dress or top. Although it is usually just a simple sash, there are some key pointers to making these belts quickly and easily. Because they are out front on the body, they should look crisp and professional.

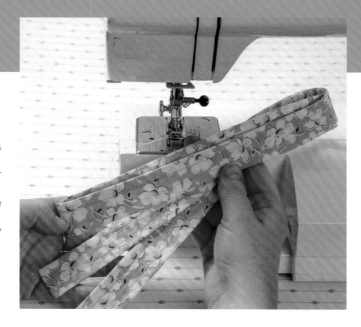

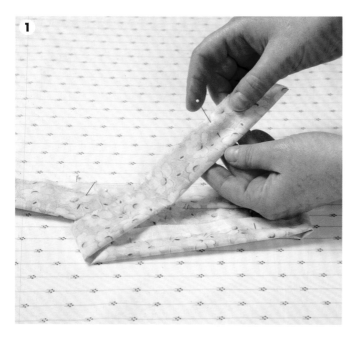

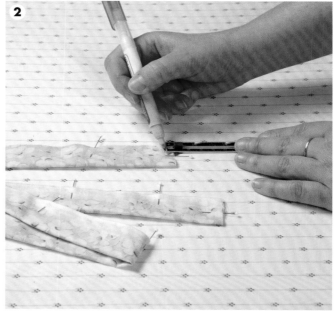

1. Cut one belt piece twice as wide as the desired width, plus seam allowance. The length should be cut to the desired amount, plus seam allowance. Fold the belt in half and pin, with right sides together.

2. To pivot at the right-angled ends, mark the pivot spots with a chalk pencil and seam gauge.

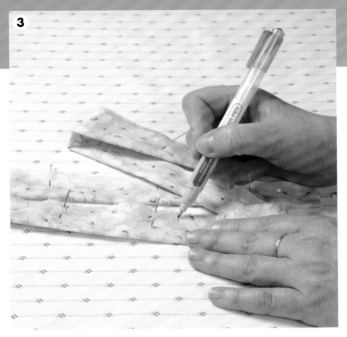

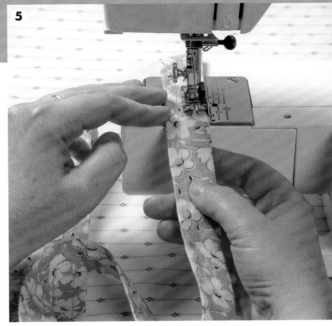

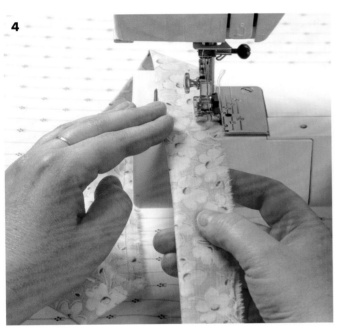

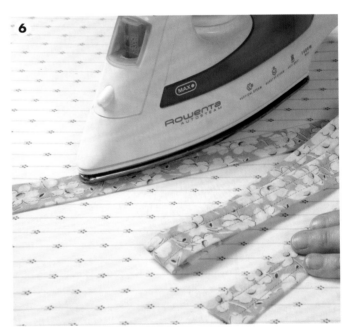

3. The center 3" (7.6 cm) will be left open, so mark 1½" (3.8 cm) on either side of the center mark along the length of the belt.

4. Sew the belt as pinned, starting at one end, pivoting at the corner, and stopping at the halfway mark. Continue from the other halfway mark to the opposite end and pivot. Trim the seam allowance down around the corners to get a clean angle when turned right-side out.

5. Turn the belt right-side out using a point turner to get crisp corners, and press with an iron. Fold the seam allowance into the opening left at the halfway mark and pin closed. Using a water-soluble chalk pencil, mark the pivot points at each end on the right side of the belt. Topstitch by sewing all the way around both long sides and each short end, closing up the opening left at the halfway mark at the same time. Starting at the center of the belt will keep any backstitching at the back of the body and not in the front at a tie's end.

6. Press the entire belt flat and set the stitches.

CONTRIBUTORS

Sarai Mitnick of Colette Patterns

Alexia Abegg of Green Bee Patterns

Tasia Pona of Sewaholic Patterns

Devon Iott of Miss Make

Marisa Anne of Creative Thursday

FEATURED FABRIC AND PATTERN DESIGNERS

Christine Haynes Patterns

Colette Patterns

Green Bee Patterns

Sewaholic Patterns

Marisa Anne and Creative Thursday for Andover Fabrics

Melody Miller for Kokka

Rob Bancroft of Green Bee for Cloud9 Fabrics

Lizzy House for Andover Fabrics

Made by Rae Patterns

Jamie Christina Patterns

Grainline Studio Patterns

Lotta Jansdotter for Windham Fabrics

Nani Iro by Naomi Ito

Denyse Schmidt for FreeSpirit

Denyse Schmidt for Joann Fabrics and Crafts

Amy Butler for Rowan

Anna Maria Horner for FreeSpirit

Anna Maria Horner Patterns

Kaffe Fassett for Westminster Fibers

Suzy Ultman for Robert Kaufman Fabrics

Alexander Henry Fabrics

Liberty of London Fabrics

Heather Ross for Kokka

Joel Dewberry for FreeSpirit

Marc Jacobs

Ralph Lauren

ABOUT THE AUTHOR

Christine Haynes learned to sew when she was ten years old and grew up in a family of seamstresses. She obtained a bachelor of fine arts from the School of the Art Institute of Chicago before launching her eponymous business. Christine has her own line of sewing patterns, writes regularly for many sewing magazines, and teaches sewing in Los Angeles and online.

Christine's work has been featured in *Threads Magazine*, *The New York Times*, *Cloth Magazine*, *The New York Post*, *The Los Angeles Times*, *Sew News Magazine*, NBC's *The Today Show*, *Sew Stylish Magazine*, the Martha Stewart Radio Network, and Daily Candy, among others. See her collection of goods at her website, ChristineHaynes.com.

Photo by Christine Haynes. Makeup by Dorit Wright.

ACKNOWLEDGMENTS

There are many to thank who helped make this book possible. Big thanks to contributors Sarai Mitnick, Alexia Abegg, Tasia Pona, Marisa Anne, and Devon Iott, some of the kindest ladies in the business, for contributing to the book. Thank you to Linda Neubauer for asking me to take on this project and to Gaby Moussa for photographing all my steps along the way. Huge thanks to the greatest family and friends who always offer me an unmatched level of love and support. I love you mom, Scott, Jenifer, Ileana, and Jennifer! Far away thanks to my late grandma Ruth, who is part of the book as her supplies and tools grace many of the pages. And the biggest thank-you goes to my love, Mike, for being everything, and then some.

Index